Beginne

BEGINNERS GUIDE TO DIGITAL MARKETING:

HOW TO FLOOD YOUR WEBSITE WITH TRAFFIC IN 30 DAYS

COPYRIGHT © 2015 ROMUALD ANDRADE

ALL RIGHTS RESERVED.

To my daughter, Erika,

You have taught me so many things:

What truly matters in life,

To find pleasure in simple things,

To find humor in any situation,

And to trust that tomorrow will be a better day.

Thank you for just being you. I am proud and happy to be your dad.

- Romuald

TABLE OF CONTENTS

SECTION 1

SECTION 2

Day 1: The Creative Brief

Day 2: The Success Tracker

Day 3: The Keyword List

Day 4: Your Domain Name

Day 5: Call To Action

Day 6: The Content Calendar

Day 7: Sources Of Traffic

PITSTOP 1

Day 8: List Building

Day 9: Google Adwords

Day 10: Google Webmaster Tools

Day 11: Google Analytics

Day 12: CRM

Day 13: Conversion Rate Optimization

Day 14: The Buying Cycle

PITSTOP 2

Day 16: Autoresponder

Day 17: Email Content
Day 18: SEO

Day 19: Facebook

Day 20: LinkedIN

Day 21: Twitter

PITSTOP 3

Day 22: Pinterest

Day 23: Google Plus

Day 24: Hootsuite

Day 25: Lead Qualification

Day 26: Reports

Day 27: Brand and Non-Brand

Day 28: Measure

PITSTOP 4

Day 29: Customer Behavior

Day 30: The Review

SECTION 3

Your Free Gift

As a way of saying, "Thanks for your purchase," I'm offering a free download of my marketing template.

This template is the exact same tool I used to help over 200 clients (of which 12 were well-known nationwide brands) to get more value out of their digital marketing efforts.

You can download this template by going here:

http://www.authorandfriend.com/brief/

If you have received some value from this Kindle book, I'd love to have a review from you on Amazon.com.

I look forward to your comments and feedback. You can send me an email at authorandfriend@gmail.com.

Who can this book help?

If you have never done digital marketing before and need a simple book that gets to the point and shows you the steps to getting it done, then this book is perfect for you.

If you have already done some form of inbound marketing but you need a framework, then this book will help you.

If you want to compress years of trial and error into days, then this book might be for you.

If you have done event marketing or print-based marketing, which means you already have a marketing base and you just want a primer in digital marketing, then this book is for you.

Or maybe you are a business owner and you need a launch a new product in the next 30 days. This book will give you the framework you need to successfully manage and keep track of the marketing aspects of your product launch.

When I started writing this book, I wrote out only the 30-day plan and I thought that I was finished. After reading through it a few times, I realized that I was making critical assumptions about you. If these assumptions were wrong, then it would render this whole book useless.

To correct this error, I have listed the things you must understand before you begin.

First off, I want you to know that I believe that you are a self-motivated person. I believe that you are doing this because you have a lot of responsibility to handle and the success of your digital marketing efforts is critical for both your company and yourself.

1. I assume that you have basic technology skills. You can use the Internet, find items in a search engine, and send an email.

2. I assume that you have a product or service or a niche that you are targeting. In other words, before doing anything else, you must know what audience you are targeting, because you cannot do marketing without having this in mind.

3. I assume you have social media accounts already established on Facebook, LinkedIn and YouTube. While I will explain what to do with these accounts, setting them up is beyond the scope of this book.

4. I assume you are taking a long-term view of your digital marketing efforts. This is important because if you are just looking for a one-off solution, then this book may not be right for you.

5. I assume that you are willing to take a calculated risk with paid media and are not looking

only for free solutions. What I have learned is that even free things cost money because there is the cost of the lost opportunity when you invest your TIME and don't get the level of results that you expect.

How To Use This Book

This book is divided into three parts.

Section 1 focuses on the prerequisites you need to have in place before you start your digital marketing activities.

Section 2 gives you a day-wise action plan. Ideally, you will follow my day-by-day instructions for the first 30 days. After the initial 30 days, you can continue to follow my day-by-day instructions or you can focus on those activities that worked better for you.

Section 3 gives you a list of resources so that it is easier for you to execute.

In addition to this book, you can visit my website, listed below; to access many other free downloads.

http://www.authorandfriend.com/brief/

How Will You Benefit From This Book?

The book is more strategic than hands-on. You will find the material organized into several categories designed to walk you through the process.

Here's just a taste of what you'll discover…

How to structure your inbound marketing efforts with a simple 30-day plan
Secrets of digital marketing management few people know about
How to bring a level of sanity to your product launch efforts in just a few short minutes
A strategic framework for the first 30 days of your marketing plan.
Marketing strategies and tactics worth $$$$$! Trust me, I have seen how much money businesses waste on marketing, and it can cost in the tens of thousands of dollars.

You're going to want to know something before you purchase this book: It's going to be a lot of work, so be prepared to allocate 30 days of dedicated time and effort to this activity.

Digital Marketing isn't always easy or clear cut at first, but with time and energy spent learning and practicing the step-by-step method I'll show you, you'll understand how to measure the performance of your team and get the results you need from your efforts on a consistent basis.

I will explain to you my own pitfalls and perils in the case study section, along with advice I found while I was looking for solutions to my own challenges when executing such projects. These should hopefully make things simpler for you, since you will not have to learn from trial and error; however, I would like to underline that just because it is simple does not mean it will be easy.

Now, this begs the question: is it worth the effort? And my answer is yes; it is definitely worth it.

I invite you to join me on this journey as we learn about Digital Marketing.

SECTION 1

My Digital Marketing Background

It's important to know who you are listening to when you get digital marketing advice. That's why I want to start with my story.

I published my first website in the year 2003. After publishing my website, I sent the link to my friends for their feedback, which resulted (eventually) in a lot of inquiries from small business owners who wanted to have websites for their own businesses. As a freelancer, I was happy to help people by creating their websites, but a few of them would come back to me after a year and say that they did not want to renew the website for the next year.

This caught me by surprise, because I would get approval from them at every stage of building the website (about six stages in total) and I would not proceed from one to another unless they had approved the previous stage. So how could it be that they were now unhappy with a website that they were ecstatic about a year earlier?

The answer was they felt that that their websites did not make money for them and were therefore a wasted expense. But on drilling down further, I realized that the websites had helped them in their branding and marketing efforts, but they did not have a way of measuring how successful their websites were.

The solution I found at the time was to install

Google Analytics on every website that I made from that point on, which led to my interest in SEO (Search Engine Optimization) followed by social media marketing and paid media. I joined an agency as a Project Manager and got a lot more exposure to digital marketing while handling marketing campaigns for multinational companies. The average number of website visits for some of these companies was about 2 million users per month.

I also developed a questionnaire, which I would ask every client to fill out before starting his or her project. This document also helped me a lot when I started working with small business owners, and I was able to offer them access to tools and help them out as a digital marketing consultant. As of now, I have successfully used the questionnaire in over 200 companies in 14 different industries, which has given me confidence that my method works.

This document is provided as a free download on my website as my way of saying, "Thanks for purchasing this book."

http://www.authorandfriend.com/brief/

Lessons Learned

Throughout this book, I'll be sharing what's worked for me and what is most likely to work for you. But three lessons stand out above the rest.

Lesson 1: Do a weekly review of your project, which I refer to as a Pitstop.

A marketing project that's not exceptionally successful is probably heading down the wrong direction because of one or more of its lead sources/channels not operating at its peak. Taking charge and checking fairly often is the key to get the plan back on the right track. A pitstop will help you do that. You need to mainly use a quantitative approach to measure your success.

Lesson 2: Get quality traffic.

Quality traffic is the key to digital marketing. By "traffic," I mean the visitors coming to your website. If these visitors don't have the intent to buy, then it is not quality traffic.

Lesson 3: Know the difference between Strategy, Tactics, and Execution.

The initial project plan used at the product launch stage usually gets hopelessly out of whack due to poor execution. (A combination of good strategy and poor execution is like a Ferrari with flat tires: it looks good in the specs, but fails on the street.) Often, people pass off tactics as strategy, and so end up skipping strategy altogether. Tactical decisions are the day-to-day decisions required for the marketing campaign, whereas strategy is generally consistent for the entire year and rarely changes.

Sometimes, you need to know which marketing activity will have the best results even before you commit to it fully. The solution is a pilot program or an experiment with a small budget before you scale up the activity.

Prerequisites

Digital marketing requires various tools and resources to be available for use depending on the activities undertaken. We will be looking at these activities in the 30-day plan; however, we need to ensure that we have a few basics in place before we undertake the 30-day plan.

There are three basic things you need to have in place before we begin.

1) A logo for each segment of your business.
2) Team members with different specialties who can prioritize and handle tasks efficiently.
3) A Gmail ID specifically created for the purpose of digital marketing. Since you might need to share this ID and password with your team, it makes sense to keep it separate from your personal or official IDs.

I will explain these in detail.

Logo

When a client approaches me and he does not have a logo or has a logo that looks like clipart, it immediately sets off alarms in my head.

To be fair to these clients, I will list some of their reasons:

1) They do not want to invest in promoting and managing multiple brands.
2) They have been using the same clipart logo for years without any problems.
3) They are just starting out so they don't know if it is worth the investment.
4) No one in their industry uses a logo.
5) They have never felt the need for a logo.

All of the above may be perfectly valid reasons, given the mindset of a non-marketing person. But as any good marketing person will tell you, you NEED to have a logo for every SEGMENT of your business.

Now before you write me off, let me explain. You can have a "Group Logo" for your main business that stays constant, but with a tagline that changes for every segment within that business. That would still give you an edge over the competition. But by no means should you try to avoid having logos for different business segments, and here are the top three reasons why:

In the process of creating a logo for your brand, you end up defining that brand or segment for your company.
You clearly associate an image of what your brand should look like or feel like to your end customer.
More importantly, you also define what your brand is NOT, or what it does not stand for.

Your Team: Should you outsource?

Outsourcing is quite popular now. But let us first understand what it is all about and whether it can work for you and your company.

Many small business owners are anxious to get started and want to start off as a one-man army. Other companies with existing in-house staff try to get their staff to execute digital strategy without really knowing if that person or persons are right for the job. There are also companies that create an in-house digital department from scratch with students fresh out of college.

Digital marketing is a relatively new industry and it can be quite challenging to find the right staff for it. The best solution is to have one in-house digital specialist and then outsource the execution to either an agency or freelance specialists. The in-house expert monitors the digital campaigns, makes sure that an integrated digital strategy is followed, and mobilizes the company's existing resources to deliver what the agency or freelancer needs.

A Virtual Team

A virtual team, or a remote team, is a team that works virtually. It is usually geographically diverse and so may never meet face-to-face. Outsourcing to a virtual team has its pros and cons.

Advantages of virtual teams:

Increased productivity. Virtual teams have flexible work schedules. With the "follow the sun" approach, a team on the other side of the globe can easily pick up where the previous team has left off.

Extended market opportunity. With geographically dispersed teams, there is direct access to different market opportunities. Organizations can establish their presence in different parts of the world through their teams, allowing small businesses to compete globally.

Knowledge transfer. Having people with varying knowledge across the globe is advantageous to any organization.

Disadvantages of virtual teams:

Communication deficiency. Humans communicate better with body language. With limited virtual communication media and Internet restrictions, misinterpretations in emails or messages may arise, which can eventually lead to failure.

Poor leadership and management. Any failure in any team, virtual or not, will boil down to poor leadership and management. However, in virtual teams, this becomes more prominent due to ineffective communication.

Incompetent team members. Due to physical distance, virtual teams are much more affected by timing when completing projects. Virtual teams must be

composed of competent members who can complete their assigned tasks on time.

Freelance marketplaces

To lessen the risks associated with a virtual team, it is better to employ the services of a freelance marketplace to manage your virtual team.

Freelance marketplaces have two user types: buyers (clients) and sellers (freelancers). Buyers register, complete a basic profile, and post projects with their requirements. Sellers bid for the projects on an hourly basis or a fixed-price basis. Once the job is done, the buyer pays the seller and provides feedback. This feedback is displayed publicly on the seller's profile.

Freelance marketplaces have rating systems to assess the skills of available freelancers. This is visible in seller profiles, along with a description of the services they offer, sample works, and sometimes their rates. Hire people based on skill rating, skill sets, and past works, not just their rates. And as with most things, the best way is to start small.

Some examples of freelance marketplaces are Odesk.com, Elance.com, Guru.com and Freelancer.com.

Your 5-Minute Digital Marketing Budget Plan

Now, let's work out a very simple budget plan so that you're on track to generate leads for your business through digital marketing.

As a rule of thumb, companies should spend between 10% to 20% of revenue on marketing.

* What is your annual revenue? _____
* 10% of that is _____. That's your annual marketing budget.
* Divide the annual marketing budget by 12 to get the monthly marketing budget.
* Divide the monthly marketing budget by 4 to get the weekly marketing budget.

Your marketing budget would be something you'll need to plan for the entire financial year, but it also is something that you need to review every week and increase when required. Twenty percent of revenue is not the maximum that a company should spend on marketing, especially if that company is a startup or if the overall economy or the industry segment is on a strong growth trajectory.

Now that your weekly budget is set, let's get into what you need to have done. You may want to revisit this section after you have finished implementing the 30-day plan.

What are the marketing activities you need to get done that <u>you can't do yourself</u>? For each one, is it a project or an ongoing process?

* _____ Ongoing / Project based
* _____ Ongoing / Project based
* _____ Ongoing / Project based

What are the marketing activities that you need to get done because <u>you shouldn't be doing them</u>? (That is, what tasks are you doing that, as the owner of the company, you shouldn't be doing?) For each one, is it a project or an ongoing process?

* _____ Ongoing / Project based
* _____ Ongoing / Project based
* _____ Ongoing / Project based

What are the marketing activities that you need to get done because <u>you don't like doing them</u>? For each one, is it a project or an ongoing process?

* _____ Ongoing / Project based

* _____ Ongoing / Project based
* _____ Ongoing / Project based

If your budget is too low for all of this right now, we'll need to prioritize.

Which item from the lists above would give you the SINGLE biggest possible return for your company if it were done?

It may be hard to pick only one, and of course no one has a crystal ball, but what is really holding your company back? Or what project would most likely boost the bottom line of your company the fastest?

In the 30-day plan that I will explain in Section 2, you will get many ideas for things that you can do to improve your marketing efforts. But just because you can do it does not mean that you SHOULD do it. After the initial 30 days of executing this plan, you will note that SOME of the activities outlined in the plan are working for your company while other activities are not. One technique that usually works very well is to stop the activities that are not working for your company and move the budget allocated to activities that are working.

The trick to doing this well is to measure, measure,

and measure. If an activity by its very nature is not measurable, then you should not do it, especially if there is a cost in terms of time, money, or personal effort involved.

SECTION 2

DAY 1: THE CREATIVE BRIEF

A common problem most clients face with digital marketing is how to get the best performance from their digital marketing team.

Are you finding it difficult to explain the idea you have in your mind to your designer so that she can get the job done?

Has your marketing team started off in the wrong direction, so you have to stop, figure out where the heck you're going, and start over?

What if you had a road map that could get you there?

A creative brief is like a road map. A great creative brief leads to persuasive marketing. This can be summarized in a simple sentence:

Don't Expect Your Marketing Team To Read Your Mind.

What is a creative brief?

In marketing, a creative brief is a document containing the instructions for the work to be done by the marketing team. The purpose of this brief is to align marketing resources, such as the copywriters, graphic designers, and others, with the client's marketing strategy. In this book, I keep using the words creative brief, marketing brief and client brief interchangeably but they all refer to the same document.

The most important part of this creative/marketing/client brief template is the list of the goals of the client. If these marketing goals are not communicated early on in the process, the marketing team can start off in the wrong direction, which leads to wasted time and wasted money. If you are a marketer and you don't know what success means to your client, then you will be lost. If you are an employee in the marketing department, then simply substitute the word "client" with "boss."

If you are a small business owner and you are reading this, you need to ensure that your money is well spent, which means that you need to explain your idea of what success would look like to your marketing team. Most small business owners I speak to have not thought this far ahead, which means that they are not clear as to what their goals should be. On the other hand, I have noted that sometimes the client *does* have a clear business goal in his/her mind, but does not articulate this goal to the marketing team. In both scenarios, it really helps to have the client fill out a questionnaire in order to get everyone on the same page. A few clients delegate this task without fully understanding what it means to the bottom line.

There is a third scenario with established companies who already have a lot of marketing materials available. Sometimes, while going through these marketing materials, it is obvious that there is confusion in the messaging. As the saying goes, "If you don't stand for something, you will fall for anything."

The main stakeholder has to be a part of this activity. If he is unable to dedicate the time, you as the marketer should take the initiative to interview him and fill out the creative brief form yourself based on his inputs.

You can visit my website listed below to download the creative brief, as well as many other free downloads.

http://www.authorandfriend.com/brief/

As an example, let's look at a few questions from the creative brief template and see how we could answer them.

Q1. Who is your target customer?
Q2. What is the target customer problem and solution in a nutshell?

Q3. What are the benefits of your solution?
Q4. What is your value proposition — the promise that will solve the target customer's problem, meet their needs, or satisfy their desires?
Q5. Why should your target customer believe your promise?

In order to answer these questions, let's assume that you are the marketing manager for Domino's Pizza:

Q1. Who is your target customer?
A1. People within a one-mile radius of each pizzeria, ages 18 and above, both male and female.

Q2. What is the target customer's problem and solution in a nutshell?
A2. There are many pizzerias, but they are all trying to either compete on price or on taste. The real problem that they ignore is that people who order pizza delivery are already hungry. The solution is to get the pizza to them fast.

Q3. What are the benefits of my solution?
A3. Two key benefits: the customer will not have to stay hungry for long and can look forward to eating a hot meal in the next 30 minutes.

Q4. What is your value proposition — the promise that will solve the target customer's problem, meet their needs, or satisfy their desires?
A4. You get fresh, hot pizza delivered to your door

in 30 minutes or less — or it's free.

Q5. Why should your target customer believe you?
A5. The target customer has nothing to lose. If the pizza is on time he wins; if the pizza is not on time, he wins.

Word-of-mouth marketing

What does word-of-mouth marketing have in common with digital marketing? I am glad you asked.

An important component of your word-of-mouth/referral strategy is your *elevator pitch*. Your elevator pitch is a 30- to 60-second presentation that can be delivered verbally with or without the use of props. In other words, you need to identify the remarkable segments/aspects of your business and then figure out how to build a story around each segment.

The elevator pitch can be also used for making videos for the purpose of digital marketing because the thought process for a viral video is essentially the same as an elevator pitch. These videos have to entice the viewer to excitedly tell a friend, "You gotta see this!" When you produce these videos the right way, they are designed to be viral in nature.

Here is a technique I learned from Dr. Ivan Misner,

founder of BNI and the Referral Institute. In his book, *"The World's Best Known Marketing Secret,"* Dr. Misner has given us a method to craft our elevator pitch by dividing it into five parts:

Introduction - what we do
The remarkable segment - the aspect of your business you want to cover
The LCD success story - elaborate further with a story, preferably a true story :)
Call to action - specific action request
Memory hook - something catchy; it does not need to rhyme but it should be memorable

The first part is fairly straightforward, but before you introduce your company, introduce the problem you will solve for your customer.

This customer should represent a niche or a segment of the population. For example, your target customer could be a doctor, a real estate agent, or a banker. When we refer to the LCD, we mean the Least Common Denominator. In this case, we have used the acronym LCD interchangeably with the target customer.

How do I identify my LCD group?
Firstly, you have to start by asking the right questions. The questions given below are more from the business owner's perspective so, if you are the marketer, do ensure that you get the following questions answered by the business owner.

1) The kind of lead that works for us is someone who…
2) The kind of lead that does not work for us is someone who…
3) We do our best work with someone who…
4) We are most interested in the type of client who…
5) What we do best is…

Once you have identified this LCD group or groups, think of the poster boy or poster girl of each group again and think of their story. What were they struggling with, and how did your company help them?

Now place the target customer (the LCD) at the center of a story about him/her. What problem is he/she facing?

The remarkable segment of your business is where you introduce your company as the knight in shining armor and show how your solution was used to solve this problem for someone very similar to the target customer or in the same situation as him or her.

Now, let us use these two components—that is, the creative brief *and* the elevator pitch—to make our first video.

The four steps to creating a great video:

1) **Identify the problem**. You need to tap into the emotions of your viewers. You should lead with a

common problem or what problem you solve.

2) **Explain the solution**. Next, mention how you'll solve that problem. It's best to keep this short and sweet so that your viewer gets it immediately. Describe the benefit you provide, not your features.

3) **Explain how it works**. This is where you elaborate on the solution and introduce some detail about your product or service. Now you can mention features, but don't forget to include the benefits of those features. Most buyers will know about your competition, so if possible, mention the factors that make you different from them.

4) **Wrap up**. This is where you mention your company and memory hook. Summarize your value proposition in one line. This should be short and memorable. Make sure you let the viewer know the next step; for example, "click on the link below" or "subscribe now."

Your script doesn't have to be laid out in this manner (after all, it is a creative process), but this is an intuitive and natural way for a viewer to comprehend an idea.

The good news is that you don't need to think about the various parts of the video since you have already have all these answers written out when you filled out the creative brief and the word-of-mouth strategy. In fact, you just might have enough material for seven or eight videos by now. :)

The steps for making a video are as follows:

\# Make a video script using the four steps given above.
\# Revise the script using the elevator pitch framework.
\# Record a voiceover yourself, or hand this script off to a voiceover artist.
\# Collect the images for the video or ask your designer to collect images based on the script.
\# Combine the images and voiceover into a video using video editing software or hand off the images with the script and the audio file of the voiceover to your video-editing specialist.

Case Study – Day 1

David owns a letting agency (PI Rentals) in Surrey, UK. A letting agent is a real estate agent who does not deal in buying and selling of properties, but only specializes in bringing landlords (who want to rent out their property) and tenants (who need a place to stay) together for a brokerage fee. David has been a landlord himself for the last 13 years, so he has a very good idea about what his target customers want.

He has two types of target customers, landlords being the first group and tenants being the second group.

David is interested in digital marketing, since he wants to grow his business. He has gone through the book *Beginners Guide to Digital Marketing* and now wants to implement the 30-day plan for his business.

He starts out with the Creative Brief questionnaire and answers the questions as follows:

Q1. Who is your target customer?
I have two types of target customers, landlords and tenants. Landlords own more than one property in the Surrey area of the UK. Tenants are looking for a property to live in within the Surrey area of the UK.

Q2. What are the target customers' problems and solutions, in a nutshell?
The landlord is looking for someone to pay him rent for his property but is worried that the tenant may not maintain the property and may hassle him for repairs. He is also worried that the tenant may not pay him on time and he might have to wait a long time to get the right kind of tenant. The tenant is looking for a good and well-maintained property within his budget in the Surrey area because he wants to live near his workplace and he wants a place which is conveniently located near his son's school.

The solution for both is our Passive Income Rental Service. Landlords can look forward to renting out their property in a timely manner. We check the credit score of the tenant as well as get him a guarantor who is willing to take responsibility for the tenant. We also draw up the necessary paperwork, keeping in mind the current laws. This is a premium service, where we take care of the property repairs with our team of civil contractors for the actual cost of the repairs and an additional fee.

Q3. What are the benefits of your solution?

The benefit to the landlord is a true passive income solution if he decides to go ahead with the premium service since we double up as a property manager and maintain the property for the landlord. The benefits to the tenant are that he gets a property within his budget and he will not need to chase the landlord for repairs.

Q4. What is your Value Proposition — the promise that will solve the target customers' problems, meet their needs, or satisfy their desires?

For Landlords: The PI Guarantee is that if your current tenant does not fulfill his legal obligations as mentioned in your contract, we will waive off our brokerage fee for your next tenant.

For Tenants: We guarantee that we will fix any broken plumbing or any other civil work within 24 hours on weekdays and within 48 hours on weekends.

Q5. Why should your target customer believe your promise?

Landlords: We will clearly mention our guarantee in a separate legal agreement that you sign with us.

Tenants: We will appoint a dedicated property manager and also give you a 24 hour helpline number for any repair related matters.

David then starts working on his elevator pitch. He would like to focus on landlords for his referral strategy, so he breaks down his elevator pitch as follows:

Introduction
Hi, I am David Smith from PI Rentals. We have been a leading letting agency in Surrey for the past 13 years.

The remarkable segment
Today, I would like to talk about my "Passive Income Rental Service."

The LCD success story
I would like to tell you a success story about one of my customers, Dr. Stephen, who is a dentist. He owns 17 properties in the Surrey area and is a very busy person. When he came to us two years ago, he was already working with seven other letting agents and he was very knowledgeable about the property market in the area. In the past two years, he has switched over a total of 12 properties to my company because he was very happy with the level of service that we provided. While he still works with other agents, he prefers *to deal with us—and has referred other doctor friends to us, too.*

Call to action
If you know a doctor who is interested in investing in passive income rental properties, please refer them

to me.

Memory hook
At PI Rentals, we put your income on autopilot.

David decides to use his video as a traffic mechanism to get more leads to his website. He decides to do an explainer animation video and writes the video script as follows:

The problem
This is Dr. Stephen. He is a busy dentist who owns some rental properties.

From the outside, Dr. Stephen's life looks ideal, but he is really tired of attending to his tenants' phone calls. They call him when he is consulting with a patient; they call him when he is in the middle of a surgery; they even have ways to get past his receptionist. Stephen needs to find a way to make this work.

The solution
Stephen meets an old friend who also owns some real estate. His friend tells him about PI Rentals, who have helped him put his rental income on autopilot.

How does it work?
Stephen calls David Smith from PI Rentals and

meets with him to discuss his options. David is friendly and helpful. He shows Dr. Stephen his Passive Income Rental Plan and his PI guarantee. He also lets him know about his fast turnaround time and his legal services.

Stephen decides to sign up with PI Rentals. Now he is able to spend more time with his family and focus on his business of helping patients while at the same time enjoying a stream of passive income from his rental properties.

Wrap up
If you own rental property in Surrey, you need to look us up. Click on the link below to sign up for a no-obligation, Free letting Valuation of your property and get all your questions answered.

Now that his script is complete, David emails the script and his logo to his video-editing specialist. He is happy that he has completed the first step of his marketing plan.

DAY 2: THE SUCCESS TRACKER

Measuring Success

On Day 2, we will look at ways of monitoring and measuring success for our digital marketing activities. To do this we need to consider four things: goals, strategies, objectives and tactics.

A **goal** is a broad primary outcome.
A **strategy** is the approach you take to achieve a goal.
An **objective** is a measurable step you take to achieve a strategy.
A **tactic** is a tool you use in pursuing an objective associated with a strategy.

What does Success look like to you?

You may have a product or a service. The product or service may have an e-commerce setup, a brick-and-mortar storefront, or a hybrid "click and brick" model. It is fair to assume that whatever the case, what you really require is sales of your product or service. Sales are done on the order page of the e-commerce site or by salespersons in the store.

The main job of the marketing team is to provide leads to the sales team. A typical digital marketing project may have one or more of the following goals.

1) Revenue
2) Branding
3) Lead Generation
4) Product or Service Sales
5) Website Visitor Conversions
6) Engagement
7) ROI – Return on Investment

You should notice that I mentioned "Product or Service Sales" as one of the goals. If this is a goal for your marketing team, then the marketing team will have to work very closely with the sales team to achieve it. A geographically dispersed team would have great difficulty in chasing this particular goal.

The formulas given below are the formulas I have seen companies using to measure the goals listed above. You may choose to measure these differently, but I have listed them here for easy reference.

1) **Revenue**. The formula for calculating revenue is (number of customers) × (number of transactions per customer) × (average ticket size).

2) **Branding**. The number of referrals from existing customers is the best metric to measure branding efforts. The number of transactions per customer is also a good indicator.

3) **Lead Generation**. The two best metrics for lead generation are the number of leads and the ROI% (return on Investment).

4) **Product or Service Sales**. The best metric to measure sales is the absolute sales number, along with the Lead-to-Sale Conversion Ratio, also known as Conversion Rate (%).

5) **Website Visitor Conversions**. Visitor Conversions is calculated as follows: Number of Clicks/Visitors, divided by the number of Leads.

6) **Engagement**. Facebook measures Engagement Rate as follows: Total Engagement (likes + comments + shares) divided by the Total Fans.

7) **ROI – Return on Investment**. ROI is one of the best methods of measuring success. A good ROI means spending one dollar and generating more than a dollar in return. A bad ROI is when you are generating less than a dollar in revenue against your marketing spend of one dollar.

My advice would be to pick only one of these goals as the goal for your digital marketing efforts. When you have to aim at a moving target or more than one target, you tend to miss most of the time.

The success criteria, however, would vary depending on the activities undertaken. For example, if engagement is a criterion for you, your best investment might be Facebook or LinkedIn, depending on your type of business.

Let us see how we can map the success of a particular marketing activity using our success criteria.

Goal
To generate 200% ROI

Strategy
To focus on traffic with buying intent

Objective
To convert 4% of leads against the current trend of 2% lead conversion

Tactics
Facebook Ads, Google Ads

Expected Outcome
Currently we are generating 1000 leads per month at 100% ROI and converting 20 leads into sales. We want to increase that to 40 sales while keeping the budget and the number of leads constant, which would be a conversion of 4% with an ROI of 200%

Case Study – Day 2

David decides to note down his success criteria but

first he has to pick a goal. He decides to consider Lead Generation as his primary goal with ROI as the secondary goal. Currently he does not have a marketing budget and his monthly revenue is erratic. For easy calculations I am considering his revenue in dollars, rather than pounds.

Annual Revenue: $600,000
10% of that is: $60,000 minimum annual marketing budget
Monthly marketing budget: $5000 per month
Weekly marketing budget: $1250 per week

Goal
To generate 1200 leads at 100% ROI per year

Strategy
To generate 1200 fresh leads via digital marketing per year

Objective
To spend $1250 per week on lead generation against 25 leads per week

Tactics
Google ads, Facebook ads

Expected Outcome
25 leads per week

DAY 3: THE KEYWORD LIST

Your next step in digital marketing should be dealing with your keywords. You basically need to think about what your target audience is typing into Google to find you so that you will be able to target them in Google and other search engines.

Keywords are the text queries entered into search engines and social networks whenever you're conducting a search. One type of keyword phrase is what is known as a long-tail keyword. A long-tail keyword is a combination of three or more words; it needs to also be incorporated into your target list because it is more niche and thus is less competitive. Nevertheless, short keywords are also important because they offer a higher volume of search traffic.

Why build a keyword list?

One of the main reasons to build a keyword list is that today's consumers are discovering brands through search engines like Google that rank websites based upon unique keyword combinations and algorithms. You can take advantage of this by optimizing your website with relevant keywords to increase the likelihood of it being ranked and found.

A lot of other platforms, like Facebook, Twitter, etc., are also utilizing keywords now, so choosing the right ones is an important part of increasing your exposure. This is especially true whenever you're creating Search Engine Optimized (SEO) content.

Although it's difficult to know precisely which keywords are going to attract the most people, there are some ways by which you can determine just how popular and competitive they will be. There are numerous tools that you can use to determine just how competitive a specific keyword is — the Google Keyword tool, Wordstream, and Wordtracker are examples. Many of these tools will also help you to come up with new ideas. When using them, you should strive for a balance between relevance, search volume, and competitiveness. Keep in mind that your first list isn't going to be perfect, so you'll want to try out different keywords to determine which will work best for you.

Of course, you will continually need to be testing, analyzing, and refining your keywords, too. This type of keyword research is an ongoing process that will need to be monitored closely. The benefit is that you'll gain valuable insights into industry trends and product demand, which in turn will help you to increase organic traffic.

Now that you have a better understanding of keywords, here's how to create a keyword list:

\# Write down 10 keywords or short phrases that are relevant to your website. Think about what your customer would type out when they're online searching for the products or services that you offer. Your business name shouldn't be included here, especially if you're a small business owner.

\# Choose your keywords based upon their difficulty and relevance. Some words are so competitive that it's almost impossible for you to rank well for them. It's in your best interest to choose less competitive keywords that are more relevant to your business. Generally speaking, the greater the search volume is for a keyword, the more competitive it is.

\# Find a balance between relevance, search volume, and competitiveness. Choose ten keywords that match your business well. Your starter list won't be perfect, so try out different keywords to see which work best for you.

Now that you have chosen your base keywords, you should hand them off to your SEO team. The same keywords can also be used for your video when you are uploading it to YouTube.

Case Study – Day 3

David calls up his SEO project manager to have a discussion about his SEO strategy. He explains that his strategy is to focus on traffic with buying intent. The SEO project manager assures him that this can be done and requests him to provide the initial list of 10 keyword phrases so that he can start his competitor research and his keyword research.

David then emails the newly created keyword list to the SEO project manager.

His list is as follows:

letting agent surrey
rent arrears
tenant eviction
tenancy deposit help
going to court for possession proceedings
find a tenant
lettings full management
rent collection lettings
tenancy agreements

\# property inventory checklist

DAY 4: YOUR DOMAIN NAME

You need to decide what niche or business category you plan to target, and then narrow it down to something very specific. Using the example of David, who is a letting agent, David has to narrow down the topic to something such as *"letting agent surrey,"* as he is targeting a very specific audience in a very specific geographical area.

If someone in the Surrey area wants to let out their property, then the chances are that they will type out "letting agent surrey" in Google. Therefore, it would make sense for David to purchase the domain name lettingagentsurrey.co.uk if it were available.

What is a domain name?

A domain name is basically the name for your website. However, owning a domain name simply gives you the ability to prevent someone else from using that name for their website until the point where you associate this domain name with a hosting server.

What is hosting?
A hosting server is also known as a web host and a company providing a hosting server to the general public is known as a hosting company. A hosting company has computers that are specially configured and permanently connected to the Internet. They allow you to place your website on their system for a monthly/annual fee so that your website can be viewed by others on the Internet.

You can purchase domain names from many places, but I would recommend keeping your domain name and your hosting separate. As an example, you can purchase your domain name from GoDaddy and have your hosting at Bluehost.

To purchase your domain name, you simply visit GoDaddy.com to see if the domain name you want is available. Enter the domain name you want, click the Next button, and you will see whether or not the name is available for you to buy. If that particular domain name is not available, then you can choose from one of the suggestions.

If the domain you want to buy is available, then you can enter some information about yourself, and then claim the domain name. It is as easy as that.

You will need to enter your billing info, and then you will want to read the terms of service, and then you can go ahead and click the Next button. Once you have done this, you will be able to create your password that you will use to log into your account.

Once you have logged into your account, you will be able to get started, which means you will be one step closer to getting your site up and running. Don't worry about what you see, since they are a lot of upsells, which can confuse newbies.

Pick A Second Domain Name

Now that I have convinced you to purchase the domain name related to your niche, can I also convince you to get a separate domain name for your brand? Now here is where a lot of people start thinking that two domain names means that they have to invest in two websites — you don't need to worry about that. Simply ask your web designer to redirect your brand domain name to your niche domain name and then set up your hosting on your niche domain name.

The next thing you will want to do is purchase a hosting plan. I would recommend Bluehost.com for your hosting plan. Bluehost will give you an option for a free domain name so you don't need to worry about actually buying the second domain name. Once you have bought your hosting plan, you could either watch a YouTube video on how to connect your domain name to your hosting plan by using something called a nameserver or you can simply hand over the usernames and passwords to your webmaster so that he can do what's necessary. It usually takes about four hours for the changes to take effect. If it is taking too long, you can use the support ticket system to raise a query to either the GoDaddy team or the Bluehost team to sort out the matter for you.

Your actual website

Now that you have purchased your domain name and associated it with your hosting, you will want to install a WordPress website on your hosting server. Bluehost has a video tutorial on how to do this, so you can use that or ask your webmaster to do the install for you.

Now, you might wonder what WordPress is and why you would need it. WordPress is a user-friendly system that allows you to update your website without you needing to learn HTML. Doesn't that sound great? Here are some more great reasons to use WordPress:

* Google loves WordPress.
* You can use themes to style your site in line with your brand.
* Your website can grow with you since WordPress

is very scale-able.

* WordPress lets you install plugins to give you more functionality.

* WordPress provides a blog by default, which means that you can have two-way communication with visitors.

* If you want to make your website mobile-ready, it is very easy to do with WordPress.

Premium WordPress Themes: What Are They?

Once WordPress is installed on your server, you will see that the default theme that appears is not very visually appealing. The solution to this is to install a premium WordPress theme. A premium WordPress theme means that the theme costs money, and most of the time it has been built by a professional web designer. Many marketing professionals use premium themes.

There are a few reasons why you should choose a premium theme. One of them is that the quality is good, far better than the free themes you will find. Premium themes are easier to use, too, in terms of editing. Lastly, the security that comes with premium themes is far better than the security that comes with free themes.

It is also worth noting that premium WordPress themes are updated regularly, as they need to be in order to keep up with new versions of WordPress. Not only are premium themes updated often, but the support you receive from the designers is second to none. Matter of fact, if you use a free theme, then you may have a hard time finding support when you need it. A person who has created a free theme is under no obligation to help you out regardless of problems that you experience with their theme. It is worth noting that the top providers of premium themes will provide Excellent support.

If you value your time, then going with a premium theme makes sense. If you run into problems with a free theme, then you could easily waste a few hours trying to figure out the answer to the problem that you are experiencing. You might find a forum where you can find someone to help you, but there are no guarantees that you will find someone who will offer to help. You could search on Google or Yahoo, but this is also a very time-consuming process and can waste many hours. If you don't think your time is valuable, then you should get a free theme. However, if you do value your time, and you want problems solved, then go with a premium theme.

There are many types of premium themes out there, so take a look at the different ones and choose the one that you like the best. The sooner you choose a theme, the sooner your site will be up and running.

A point to note here is that each theme is different, so you may need to learn how the theme is set up. Usually, premium theme developers like WooThemes provide support (video) tutorials on how to navigate the various features of the theme. Some of theme options allow for the upload of a custom *logo* or *favicon*, and there's a section to paste some code for Google Analytics to track website visitors.

Now, let us learn and understand what Google Analytics is and why we need it.

Setting up Google Analytics on your website

Google Analytics is a tracking system provided by Google that is free to use. It helps website owners learn what is driving leads/sales to their website.

You can get your personalized Google Analytics code by creating an account at http://www.google.com/analytics/

Just follow the step-by-step instructions on the Google Analytics website.

Once you have created your personalized Google Analytics code, you can pass it to your webmaster so that he can do what's necessary.

Other Hosting Options

If you do not want to host your site through Bluehost, then you might want to do it through GoDaddy, as they have many more extensions to choose from. There are also a lot of other hosting providers out there for you to choose from. I prefer a Linux-based hosting service and not a Windows-based hosting service but that is a personal preference, since wordpress now also works on a windows based hosting service.

Case Study – Day 4

David receives his final video from his video-editing specialist.

He proceeds to upload the video on YouTube. In the description field, he places the script he has written for the video with a link to his website. He uses the keywords from his keyword list as tags for the video, as well as the title of the video. Next, he uses the share feature of YouTube to share the video on Facebook as well as his other social media channels.

When he checks his email, he is pleasantly surprised to note that his SEO team has already sent him the advanced keyword list, competitor research, and the keyword research. The information is organized into Excel sheets, but as he studies the details further, he realizes that there is a lot of information and he finds himself a bit overwhelmed, so he calls up his project manager to discuss the same.

The SEO project manager suggests that David

should follow the color-coded system usually known as "traffic lights," which uses red, yellow, and green highlighters to highlight the cells of the Excel sheet. David requests him to do what's needed and send him the modified Excel sheets when done.

On receiving the Excel sheets back, David is happy to note that each sheet has been divided into three color codes: Green for High-Priority Keywords (traffic with buying intent), Yellow for Medium-Priority Keywords, and Red for Low-Priority keywords.

He decides to focus on the green High Priority Keywords in the short term for the next 30 days and the yellow medium priority keywords for the long term and to ignore the low priority keywords for now.

David purchases the domain name lettingagentsurrey.co.uk from GoDaddy and decides to use Bluehost as his hosting provider. He notes that Bluehost provides a free domain with every hosting, so he decides to buy pirentals.co.uk.

He then proceeds to create his personalized Google Analytics code by visiting http://www.google.com/analytics/ and following the instructions.

Next, David picks up a premium WordPress theme from WooThemes and downloads the files given to him. He then emails these files and his logo to his webmaster with his login details for GoDaddy and

Bluehost so that he can set up his website for him.

The webmaster sets up the WordPress website on lettingagentsurrey.co.uk with a redirect from pirentals.co.uk and sends the WordPress login details to David. David now proceeds to change the passwords for his GoDaddy account, Bluehost account, and WordPress website as a security measure.

David notes that the theme he has purchased has a separate section for Google Analytics. He pastes the Google Analytics code in the box provided and logs into his Google account to check if it has been set up properly. He uses the Google wizard to check his website and is happy to see that the Google Analytics code has been successfully embedded into his website.

DAY 5: CALL TO ACTION

You may have noticed that some ads capture your attention.

* Get Married for Less than $5,000
* Low-Fat Fare
* Pro Fitness Guide

What makes these ads stand out? They literally entice you to click on them. A call to action is not about simply presenting a "buy now" button. What reason are you giving your visitors to invite them to subscribe, purchase, move forward, or click to view additional content?

In order to have a successful call to action, you need to:

* Explain what is in it for the visitor.
* Remove bland statements from your ads.
* Create more active buttons.
* Test simple messages for conversions.

From just an initial glance at your pages, determine the most critical information on the page. It would also help to bring in a third party to get an unbiased opinion of the messaging of your marketing, the purpose and clarity of the tagline, and the arrangement of the content and images on the page.

Evaluate your contact forms and your usage of them. Are they asking the right questions for the right conversion point? Are they too long? Do they have too many required fields? Do you really need to ask all that information in order to get the contact?

Afterward, look at your landing page after the conversion. What does it say? What can you do to provide follow-up after the conversion that will assist in building a relationship with the new customer or in moving along the sales cycle?

You want people who visit your site to DO SOMETHING. Compelling people to take action is vital if you want to generate leads, get phone calls, make sales, raise donations, or achieve whatever goals you have set for your digital marketing efforts.

Case Study – Day 5

David starts out Day 5 by outlining the sales path for his ideal customer. He figures that his ideal customer would land upon his blog, read an article or two, and become interested in subscribing to his newsletter for more articles.

He's also considered that some of them might prefer

a concise PDF report about passive income lettings in exchange for giving out their email address.

Since he has two different sales paths in mind, he names them Path1 and Path2:

Path1:
Prospect searches on Google for topic
Prospect clicks on the link
Prospect lands on website and reads article
Prospect fills out the newsletter signup form

Path2:
Prospect searches on Google for "passive income letting"
Prospect clicks on the link
Prospect lands on website and reads article
Prospect fills out the newsletter signup form

David realizes that he does not have a PDF report on passive income lettings ready, so he emails one of his virtual assistants to research the topic for him. He also emails his graphic designer regarding the cover for the PDF report.

He also decides that he needs to create "call to action" buttons for each sales path:

Path1:
* Subscribe Now
* Click Here to Subscribe Now
* Learn More

Path2:
* Get the Free Report
* Download Now

He emails these call-to-action ideas to his graphic designer to convert them into buttons.

DAY 6: THE CONTENT CALENDAR

The importance of content in Digital Marketing

For me, digital marketing is not just about providing content. It's also about branding your business, generating leads, and focusing on leads that convert to sales.

Here are some guidelines to help you create effective content.

Consider the goals of your business
Decide on a company image
Build a word-of-mouth marketing plan
Develop a content strategy
Create an escalation matrix for negative reviews
Form a content calendar
Create a comment plan
Connect CTA (calls to action) to all content

A well-organized marketing campaign is likely to be effective. The guidelines above are self-explanatory; however, they don't work in isolation. They need to be a part of the overall marketing strategy.

The Advantages of Developing a Content Calendar

The content calendar is a shareable resource used to plan content activity. Utilizing a content calendar enables the digital marketing team to plan ahead. Most teams use the calendar for forward planning, to help to line up fresh content, and to ensure that sufficient content is lined up ready to publish. Forward planning enables companies to brand their business effectively.

Identify your Audience

Your business will try to reach out to numerous types of customers, and these clients will inevitably be interested in different kinds of content. Digital agencies produce unique content for potential clients; however, they also strive to develop content that helps a business stand out above all others. So, how do you identify your audience?

Those who are marketing goods or services should listen to all client-facing employees. Meet with customer service, sales, and marketing and gather a consensus of opinion. Focus on creating varied content that generates leads.

Take Stock of Content Assets

Plenty of businesses have a wealth of valuable content stored away. You may own innumerable content marketing assets that have been set aside. Slide decks used in training sessions could be reused as blog posts, online slide decks, or videos. Data retrieved from the CRM system, finance department, or surveys can be transformed into news stories or infographics. Whitepapers can be rewritten to form a series of blog posts and older blog posts can be updated using fresh and current information.

Savvy marketers work tirelessly to brand their business, and they are aware that creative content is an essential part of any successful marketing campaign. Every successful digital marketing plan relies on fresh content. Developing a content calendar helps you to notice the window of opportunity and publish at the right time.

Marketing and planning go hand in hand. Fail to plan and you may see little return on investment. Sound marketing plans are filled with innovative ideas, and a business that is able to come up with fresh and interesting content reaches out to a wider audience. Develop a drumbeat approach to content development to connect fully with your audience and add fresh and intriguing content to keep your loyal band of followers enthralled.

To summarize, content calendars are important because they:

Help you focus on the needs of your audience
Help you inspire and connect with your audience

Help you provide value to your audience
Force you to think further than today and tomorrow
Help you integrate across mediums
Leverage, across mediums, different audiences
Create once, use many times (= increased ROI)
Streamline resources
Drive internal teamwork
Fuel idea generation and innovation
Help set expectations with your audience
Help you create loyal brand evangelists

Case Study – Day 6

David is pleased to receive some good ideas from his virtual assistant for the PDF report on passive income lettings. He decides to outsource the creation of this report to his virtual assistant with a few comments on the flow of the PDF report. He also receives the cover page design from his graphic designer, which he promptly emails to his virtual assistant to be integrated into the PDF report.

David now decides to update the content of his website. He proceeds to YouTube, where he looks for YouTube videos on how to update WordPress websites. Next, he looks up the WooThemes support area for additional information about his premium theme.

Starting with a pen and notepad, David jots down his content goals first. His main content goal is to attract landlords in the Surrey area to his website, since he would be easily able to get tenant leads by putting up the property listing on a bigger portal.

Since David has been a landlord himself, he understands that landlords worry that tenants may not maintain the property and may hassle him for repairs. They also worry that tenants may not pay on time and they might have to wait a long time to get the right kind of tenant.

He decides to focus his content not just on his passive income rental service, but also on legal tips and things he has learned from experience. He decides to focus 80% of the time on content that is informative and useful, which would establish him as an expert, and 20% of the time on sales-focused content.

He decides to write his articles in the tone of a chatty next-door-neighbor.

He currently has two virtual assistants who help him with research and content, so he decides to prepare a content calendar to ensure they put up some content every three days, which he can then approve and publish on the website.

He decides to use his keywords strategically by utilizing the high priority keywords provided by his SEO team in the title of every blog post that he puts up. He notes that WordPress makes this easy for him, since WordPress provides a blog by default, which makes his website a blog, too.

He starts off with a content calendar for just one month with a theme for each week. His theme for Week 1 is legal issues; the theme for Week 2 is easy tips for property maintenance; the theme for Week 3 is the Surrey area itself and where to find the best deals in Surrey; and his theme for Week 4 is rental rate negotiations.

He emails the basic content calendar to his virtual assistants for their feedback and inputs to start off.

DAY 7: SOURCES OF TRAFFIC

What is the one important thing that's needed to make money online?

Many online marketers believe that the only way to make money online is having a lot of traffic to their websites. But this is not entirely correct. As much as an online marketer needs people or visitors, he or she must also build trust with the visitors and also ensure lasting relationships. You can make money online only when you can convert your traffic to a sale and that sale into repeat sales.

We also know that not everyone who comes to the website will buy from you. So, it is important to know where people are coming from — in other words, the sources of your traffic. When you are able to track your traffic sources, you will know which of them convert to sales and which do not.

There are many sources of traffic that can be tracked using Google Analytics, including:
Organic Search Traffic
Referrals
Social Media marketing
Email Marketing

\# Paid Search
\# Direct Traffic
\# Dark social traffic

Organic Search Traffic doesn't come just from search engines. You need to take your keywords into consideration here so you know where your traffic, leads, and customers are really coming from, so that you can develop better-informed content strategies. This is difficult today because of Google's SSL encryption, whereby keyword information is now encrypted or hidden. This makes it a lot harder to understand which of your keywords and terms are working.

Referrals as a marketing tactic can mean a lot of different things. This is because we define a referral as any website that sends traffic to you through inbound links. As such, different software and tools track different things here. For instance, they may or may not include social media websites and subdomains. This information is important whenever you're trying to determine which web properties are of benefit to you when it comes to co-marketing, SEO partnerships, and guest blogging opportunities.

Social media marketing is another important traffic source. It not only includes someone finding your website through a social networking link, but it also includes someone tweeting out a link to your website or posting a link to your website on their Facebook page. Whenever you engage in this type of marketing, you should make sure to add a tracking token to make it easier for you to analyze everything later on. Some other important sites to remember to use here include Reddit, Tumblr, Digg, StumbleUpon, and Squidoo.

Email marketing needs to always include links back to your website. These links need to include tracking tokens so that you can know where the person is coming from when they view your link. The nice thing about this type of marketing is that you'll be able to see just how much traffic is being sent to your website from your campaign.

Paid Search marketing, or a PPC campaign, allows you to track how much website traffic is being driven to you. This is found in a report from the website where you're purchasing your clicks. You'll want to pay close attention to this report to make sure that this traffic is actually converting, so make sure to always include tracking tokens.

Direct traffic is the traffic that arrives at your website outside of one of the aforementioned channels. For instance, whenever you type in your domain URL and hit enter you arrive at your website through means of direct traffic. In other words, there's no referring URL here so whenever you see an increase in your direct traffic you can be happy that the number of people who know you by name is increasing.

Dark social traffic may also fall under the category

of direct traffic. This is traffic that a lot of analytics programs can't capture since it lacks referral data. Typically, it comes from things like emails and instant messenger programs. Just how much of this traffic you actually receive will somewhat depend upon how diligent you are in using tracking IDs. The good news is that this type of traffic should decrease more and more over the course of time.

Tracking your traffic sources

Regardless of what type of marketing you are doing, you should always make sure to create tracking links so you know what your traffic sources are.

When you're ready to create a tracking URL, you will discover there are a lot of programs online today that will help you do so. One such tracking software is Bitly. Bitly.com is free, easy to use, and provides tracking statistics that you'll be able to keep an eye on.

First of all, you'll need to set up an account. Then you can follow these steps to create a Bitly tracking link:

Let's assume we are tracking the traffic from our YouTube video.

Open a tab in your browser and search for the YouTube video that you uploaded earlier.
Open a second tab in your browser and log into

your Bitly account.

\# Open a third tab in your browser and open up your website.

\# Select the URL of your website in your browser.

\# Paste this code into Bitly to create your new link.

\# Make sure that you add a note to the link inside of Bitly so that you will be able to remember exactly what you are using this link for. The note can be something as simple as "YouTube Video1"

\# Copy and paste your new, shortened Bitly link into the description field of the YouTube video with a call to action text, such as "click here to learn more."

In conclusion, the main aim of digital marketing is to make money. If you know where your money is coming from, then you know where to get more of it.

Case Study – Day 7

David starts out Day 7 by calling his SEO project manager to discuss the tracking requirements. David feels that in order to track things properly, the tracking should be integrated with the CRM system, but the SEO project manager advises him that there is no easy way to do this.

Instead, David decides to then focus on a few areas he feels are important. Mainly, he wants to use his website as a hub, with his traffic sources being the spokes of his hub-and-spoke model.

He instructs his virtual assistant to create separate tracking URLs for two main areas, which are email marketing and social media marketing, so that it is easier to track the results of the efforts put in for these two areas. This would also give him a secondary level of analytics, apart from Google Analytics.

He proofreads the draft copy of the PDF report and suggests a few changes to his virtual assistant. When the changes are done, he emails the report to his graphic designer so that she can combine the text and graphics into one PDF report.

PITSTOP 1

David creates his Success Tracker in Excel with the following details:

Weekly budget: $1250 per week
Lead target: 25 leads per week
Appointment target: 15 appointments per week
Sales target: 1 sale per week

Since he has not yet done Google ads or Facebook ads, he has not used up any of his ad budget and he also does not have any leads for this week.

DAY 8: LIST BUILDING

The key to list building lies in offering a "lead magnet" on a "squeeze page" with an "autoresponder." What do all of these terms really mean, though?

To begin with, you should know that a lead magnet is a small PDF report that a person will download after they have given you their email address. This is typically found on a "squeeze page," which is a webpage that isn't linked to your main website.

The squeeze page works by using an *autoresponder*, which is software that's been set up to automatically send an email to someone who's filled out the lead capture form. This works by simply embedding a few lines of HTML code from the autoresponder software into your website.

Whenever you're trying to create a lead magnet, you should consider the one thing that you want to help people solve. Maybe you are an expert on real estate. Maybe you are an expert on dog training. This should be put into some type of an outline from which you will be able to write an appealing report. Once this is done, it's simply a matter of distributing it.

Keep in mind that your lead magnet doesn't have to be a full ebook. It can be:
An excerpt for a book you've written
A short video that demonstrates a concept
Some type of audio
An illustration offering a visual solution
Some type of software

How does the traffic funnel work?

First, you must have at least three sources which can help convert visitors to subscribers and then place them in the funnel.

The first is a **blog**, which has two main tasks: to provide fresh and useful content to visitors and to capture their names and email addresses. Always having fresh, useful content will ensure that first-time visitors return to the blog and even share the content via social networks.

The second source is the **squeeze page**. The main function of this page is to get names and email addresses from people.

Last is the **Facebook fan page**, with a "Like Gate" or a "Fan Gate" utilizing the TabSite app. This is a repeat of the squeeze page, but it will allow a person to collect names and email addresses from individuals visiting the fan page.

A lasting relationship cannot be built with just few visits to the website. A marketer needs to get hold of the emails of as many visitors as he can. How do you go about getting the email IDs of people visiting your website? The answer to this is having an excellent lead magnet.

A lead magnet is content on your website that helps people yet persuades them to leave their names and email addresses. This content can be a case study, video, or PDF report. After visitors leave their details in the website, they will get into your funnel. From that point, you can then begin building connections and trust, and after that, marketing products to these people can be possible.

After creating all those lead magnet pages, next is ensuring they get traffic. This can be through a variety of ways, namely Google Ads, Twitter, YouTube, search engine traffic, solo ads, and the Facebook fan page. With a constant flow of subscribers into the funnel, the marketer should get subscribers involved by encouraging them to share the page, ask questions, or comment.

When marketing your product, you should go to lengths to ensure the product really helps people. By doing this, you will be building your credibility with the buyers.

Why offer a free gift on your website?

In the past, it was easy to entice people to sign up to mailing lists; sadly, this is no longer the case. However, offer an incentive for visiting and they may show interest. Common incentives include a free niche-focused PDF report or another kind of free gift.

Imagine you had thirty days to entice one thousand people to sign up to your site. How are you going to achieve this?

Create a Fast and Unique Marketing Report as a giveaway gift.

Visit the EzineArticles homepage. Type the primary keyword into the search box on the page. This search will uncover a wealth of suitable niche-related articles. Select one or two articles that are informative and enjoyable. You can use these articles to create the basis for a free marketing report; however, you should ensure the author details remain intact. Copy and paste the article into a Microsoft Word document, add a unique introduction, export to PDF format, and you have successfully created a free marketing report.

Squeeze Pages

A mailing list is a subtle but useful marketing tool. Create interesting marketing reports that readers look forward to receiving and your business will thrive. Fail to market your business and your earnings will nosedive.

Regardless of what type of lead magnet you choose to create, you'll need to also create a squeeze page for it. This page will need to have a memory hook, which should tell people why they need this product.

Remember, the goal of your squeeze page is to obtain the visitor's email address. Any distractions could cause them to leave, which is why there shouldn't be any other links. This goal has a huge reward for you as a digital marketer, because once you have a person's email address, you'll have numerous opportunities to present them with multiple sales messages.

You need to ensure that the Google Analytics code you created earlier is embedded not just into your main website, but also into your squeeze pages.

Today, you can easily find a lot of free HTML templates for creating squeeze pages. Even professionals tend to use them, because there are a lot of benefits to doing so, including:

1) They are quicker to create because you simply need to fill in the blanks. There's no coding or technical stuff involved.
2) They have a professional look even if you aren't an expert web developer.
3) They're cheaper than creating your own or purchasing a custom squeeze page.

Choosing the right autoresponder

Part of putting together your squeeze page has to do with choosing the right autoresponder. This can actually be the difference between success and failure, which is why you want a service with proven deliverability, such as GetResponse or AWeber. While these aren't the cheapest autoresponders, they are the most successful. Furthermore, they allow you to confirm not only that your mails have arrived, but also that they have been opened, even telling you when.

By including a Bitly tracking link in your email that points to your website, you'll be able to get a secondary level of tracking, apart from the tracking provided by your autoresponder software.

Case Study – Day 8

David starts out Day 8 by looking for an autoresponder solution for his business. He finally settles on GetResponse and studies the videos provided to start with his listbuilding activities. He follows the steps required to generate the embed code for his squeeze page.

He receives the completed PDF report from his graphic designer and is happy with the final results. Next, he writes out the content for his squeeze page and emails the content, the PDF report and the embed code to his webmaster so that he can do what's necessary. His webmaster emails him back mentioning the fact that a few call-to-action graphics are required on the squeeze page. David forwards the email to his graphic designer to handle that.

David then enters the first and second emails that will go out into the autoresponder software.

DAY 9: GOOGLE ADWORDS

Google AdWords is paid advertising where you pay Google to place an ad for you in the search engine results page. When people click on your ad, they come to your website and Google is paid on a per-click basis. This is also known as PPC (pay-per-click) ads or SEM (search engine marketing).

When it is managed and set up properly, Google AdWords is one of the better sources for new customers. A few years ago, I assisted a business with their growth to earn $4 million with AdWords campaigns. But, I have also watched businesses waste tens of thousands of dollars because they did not have properly managed AdWords campaigns.

Here are some steps that will help you get started with AdWords:

Competitor Intelligence

Carefully study the companies bidding on keywords through AdWords. Find out who ranks at or near the top of the rankings on a consistent basis by using a spy tool such as iSpionage. Note the offers and ad copy that they use, and check out their websites. Sign up to get on their mailing lists, and buy their products.

Customer Demand

It is important to find out where your potential customers are reviewing businesses, services, and products like yours. Read the reviews as much as possible. Determine what it is that they hate and love about your competition, and the deep desires and needs that they would like to have fulfilled. Look out for some quotes that you can utilize in your ad copy.

Create Amazing Landing Pages

Including an awesome offer on your landing page will help to overcome any deficiencies that you may have in your AdWords campaign. You have seen what your competitors are offering, so figure out if you can offer something that is better or unique.

Use Exact Match Keywords

When you are first starting out with AdWords, keep the keyword list to only about 5 to 10 keywords. Create Exact Match keywords, which will ensure that your ads would be displayed only when the user types that exact set of keywords in the same order that you intended. Eliminate keywords that are not getting conversions or clicks, and expand on ones that are.

Group your keywords into ad groups that are closely related and based upon the intent of the searcher. For instance, keywords such as "purchase" and "buy" show that the prospect is closer to buying. The landing pages and advertisements should be focused more on closing the sale.

Stick with Relevant Ads

The ad copy must be highly relevant to the keywords, reflect the messaging and offer on your landing page, and stand out from the competition. Find out what works the best and then stick with it so that AdWords can guide your marketing engine.

Other steps necessary for you to take include creating a budget for your AdWords campaign, re-marketing towards individuals who have expressed interest in purchasing from you, and figuring out your AdWords account structure. You also will want to sign up for conversion tracking through Google AdWords. You will be able to view what keywords have value.

Create several ads to run at once, and check on the account frequently. Hopefully, this has helped you to start your own campaign to increase traffic, your sales, or your brand.

Case Study – Day 9

David starts out Day 9 by studying the keyword research and the competitor research that was sent to him by his SEO team. He reviews his budget, which is

$1250 per week on lead generation against 25 leads per week.

He also studies the remarketing plan that he has received from his PPC consultant. He is surprised to learn that he can use remarketing tactics to bring an original visitor back to his website and convert him into a paying customer. He is pleased with the idea that he can convert lost visitors via remarketing on Google AdWords.

He starts out with an AdWords plan based on the template provided to him by his PPC consultant. He assumes he will have to generate at least 50 clicks per week to get 25 leads. Therefore, he decides that the maximum bid price should be $6 per click, assuming that he would get about 16 clicks per week from Google AdWords. The PPC consultant has already set up the basic AdWords and remarketing campaigns for him and David gives him a go-ahead for the ad budget.

The PPC consultant reviews the squeeze page that has been created and suggests that at least five more squeeze pages are required. David gives the squeeze page URL to his virtual assistant and gives him five topics for the new squeeze pages to be created and asks him to create the content for the new squeeze pages.

DAY 10: GOOGLE WEBMASTER TOOLS

"Indexing" refers to the way Google classifies and catalogues your website. Google does this indexing by using a program named Googlebot, which indexes your website by "crawling" the website. "Crawling" is the term used to describe how Googlebot moves from one page of your website to another.

Typically, a website that can't get crawled has a problem with it. This could be programming, scripts, or even changes that have been made. Sometimes, there's spammy code in it that was used for marketing to search engines. The solution for spammy code is to make a "reconsideration request" to Google once the code is fixed.

Google Webmaster Tools are a great way to diagnose, track and receive important Google alerts. This is a set of tools from Google that shows how often your site is crawled, what pages are downloaded and if there's anything that's not being found. You'll also receive information about your site's rank, click-throughs and keywords to help you understand how your website is performing.

These tools are a great resource that Google is continually updating and improving upon. As such, you should be looking at it on a monthly basis, because if your website does well in Google, it will do well in other search engines, too.

Apart from this, the most important functionality provided by Google Webmaster Tools is the ability to find out what keywords have been typed in Google by the prospect in order to lead him to your website.

If you're redesigning your website, this tool will also help you to find pages that Google has "lost." This is particularly important if you're not using a redirect. It allows for a smooth transition from your old website to your new one.

Within the page-not-found report, you'll find the broken links on your site. By checking this weekly, you'll know of any linking issues before there's a problem, depending upon your level of activity on the website.

The crawl stats will show you how often the Googlebot is visiting your website to download new versions of your pages. Sometimes, this happens multiple times per day or thousands of times a month.

Whenever Google isn't crawling your website, there are some issues. The primary one is that there aren't any incoming links from reputable websites, which is the primary way in which search engines find new websites. If your website is being crawled but there aren't a lot of pages being updated or downloaded, then there may be some programming issues. Keep in mind that just because your website is crawled and indexed by the search engines doesn't mean that you're going to automatically rank well, because there are numerous factors that affect rankings.

Under the Search Queries tab in Google Webmaster Tools, you'll find a great idea of how visible your website is. Herein you'll find the keywords that were used for finding your website and how many times for each. You'll also learn how many click-throughs your listing has attracted for that keyword and the average position for this keyword. Simply organize this report based upon either Avg. Position or Click-Through Rate (CTR) so that you can see the highest-ranking words in comparison to your click-through rate.

If you find that most of the keywords are either your company or your brand name, then you need to work on your SEO. This will help to improve your rankings to ensure that people who aren't your existing clients will be able to find you.

It is important to take time to research keyword relevance to make sure that you're being found. You don't want misleading or irrelevant terms. Google Webmaster Tools will help with this.

Case Study – Day 10

David is quite happy with his progress so far and he logs in to Google Webmaster Tools to check the keyword traffic. He is pleased to note that there are no crawl errors. He is surprised, however, to see that the keyword sources are not being tracked and calls up his SEO project manager to discuss the matter. The project manager explains that until sufficient traffic volume is received on his website, Google will not display the keyword search queries. David is quite disappointed to hear this, but he is reassured that since he has just recently begun his AdWords campaign, it will just be a matter of time before the keyword data is populated within Webmaster tools.

DAY 11: GOOGLE ANALYTICS

A few days ago, you embedded a few lines of HTML code provided by Google Analytics into your website. By now, you should already have gotten a few visitors to your website, which will provide some data that can be viewed by visiting the following URL and logging in:

http://www.google.com/analytics/

Whenever you first view your Google Analytics report, you'll encounter page view information. This is data, which is value neutral — it is simply facts. In order to gain a better understanding of it, you must associate it with other data in order to add context and thus create information. In other words, by associating these numbers with an action, you can start to develop a powerful mental image that allows you to see the trends and activities taking place at your website every day. By continually adding more data, you continue to create additional levels of the information hierarchy. By synthesizing the data that you have, you're able to create knowledge about your website's visitors and their activity, which results in revenue.

However, this is the part where Google Analytics ceases to be helpful. While Google Analytics is a great tool by which you will be able to gain knowledge about the effectiveness of your digital marketing activities, it takes something more to be able to apply that knowledge and make it useful. This "something more" is you, the analyst. Once you gain knowledge about your marketing activities, you will arrive at an understanding. While analytics software can provide you with answers, it won't provide you with understanding. It is up to you to know what to do with the knowledge that you have been given.

After you have understanding, then comes wisdom. This is what happens when you know what to do to make improvements, conduct analysis, and gain additional insights. Google Analytics is only as good as the person who gets the information. For this reason, you need to invest in yourself. Otherwise, you may be wasting a lot of time on generating reports that nobody truly understands how to use. It really is up to you to look at the context in which the numbers are provided to you. Take the time to look at the search terms that a certain group of visitors used. In doing so, you will be able to develop a context, a story, and a hypothesis that you can then evaluate, judge and make decisions about.

After you develop this context, you can start to build a powerful new way to view your website's data. In doing so, you are moving beyond numbers and into the context of behavior. This makes you more of a psychologist rather than an analyst. The better you're able to understand your visitors — their intentions, their reactions, and the results of their visits — the better you'll be able to improve your digital marketing. This is because you need to know your visitors' motivations, expectations and reactions in order to be able to explain their behavior.

The result of this explanation will be better testing, optimization and ideas. All of this results from focusing on a small group of specific visitors instead of trying to improve upon a large, unfocused group.

Case Study – Day 11

David starts out Day 11 by logging into Google Analytics and studying the dashboard. He notes that most of his traffic is coming in from YouTube from the videos that he has uploaded.

DAY 12: CRM

Now that most of your digital marketing tools are set up and running smoothly, it is time to invest in a data capture mechanism. Customer relationship management software, or CRM, can help to capture data about your prospects and track their journey from a prospect to a customer. However, CRM is more than just software. As the name suggests, customer relationship management is customer-centric strategy for optimizing customer satisfaction, revenue, and profits.

Better understanding of your customers will result in easier targeting of new prospects and boosting sales. When the marketing database, sales pipeline, and customer data are routed through the CRM system, it becomes possible to monitor customer relationship and have an accurate assessment of ROI. Secondly, when data is used effectively, it becomes easier to generate sales from existing customers, and the company ends up spending less money for attracting new customers.

Any business would want to maximize its marketing leads, customers, and return on investment. These basic goals are quite attainable provided the company is able to simplify its communication channel processes, which would make it possible to derive and measure CRM benefits.

Integration is the Mantra for Optimization

It is important for marketers to know what revenue their campaigns are generating, and this is possible only through integration of order management, sales, and marketing processes. It is very important to know ROI and which channels are functioning optimally. Integration will be able to deliver a flow of the most useful information to entrepreneurs. Additionally, an integrated system of CRM will enable the company to maximize efficiency by leveraging online business, which is incorporated into the center of business activity rather than a standalone initiative.

With the rapid technological development of marketing software, it is possible now to target specific audiences with focused messages, with better reach, and with more frequency. However, this effectiveness decreases over time due to posting of messages that could be irrelevant, confusing, or downright conflicting. Such noise dilutes deliveries and overexposes the audience, resulting in failure to connect. However, new CRM software can meet such marketing challenges and provides much more than capturing customer information and its management. Today, CRM solutions can synthesize, create, and correlate data and present it in a way that makes it easy to identify relationships, patterns, and new opportunities for selling.

You have already created a marketing campaign and identified prospects and target audiences. Now it is time to select the product that you are planning to sell, design a message that will connect the need for your product with your target audience, and choose a medium for delivering this message or set of messages.

The medium (also known as a touchpoint) could be emails, phone calls, voice broadcasts, and so on. Your CRM software will be able to track how often a prospect has been contacted and which of the touchpoints has been the most effective.

A good CRM system can
Create messages
Compose target lists
Automate and schedule the distribution of messages
Capture inquires and replies
Route replies to the correct department
Track the progress of sales opportunities
Record sales
Calculate ROI from the campaign

CRM systems are now able to deliver so much because marketing list management can be integrated with the company's internal financial system and external email services. In addition, many CRM systems, such as Ontraport and Infusionsoft, now incorporate an email-marketing engine. The CRM system of today is not a passive tool for collecting customer data, but an advanced tactical tool that provides business intelligence and helps create effective marketing strategies.

Case Study – Day 12

David starts out Day 12 by checking his email. He is surprised to see that his inbox is full of inquiries from new customers. David is a bit worried about how he is going to handle all the inquiries, so he checks to see if his virtual assistant can start calling each lead and setting appointments for him.

To get things streamlined, David starts looking for a CRM solution, which could help him manage these leads. After some research, he finally settles on Nimble CRM, which has the features that he was looking for. He forwards the emails one by one to his virtual assistant, who enters each inquiry as a lead into the CRM system and then starts calling the prospects.

Two of the prospects are keen to meet him today, so David checks his Google Calendar and sets up the appointments himself.

DAY 13: CONVERSION RATE OPTIMIZATION

The word "conversion" is important in the marketing as well as the business world, and it is important to you because the purpose of your website is to convert prospects into customers. Conversion can mean different things to you, such as getting someone to buy something, register, download, sign a lead form, click an ad, or subscribe. Each conversion is designed to make your business more profitable.

You should run a minimum of two Conversion Rate Optimization (CRO) tests per month. CRO is done to improve the profit you make per visitor. Think of it this way: If you're spending $1,000 per month to drive visitors to your site, and only 1% of your visitors make a purchase (or contact you), that's a cost of $10 per sale (or lead). If you can get 2% of the same traffic to take the same action, you've just doubled your income (or leads) without spending a dime more! Plus, you've cut your cost to acquire a customer (lead) in half.

You need to think about what your website's primary goals are. What is the purpose of your site? What action or actions do you want visitors to take on your site? Then, figure out what your secondary goals are. In other words, if visitors do not do the main thing you want them to do, then what is the second thing you would prefer them to do? If a visitor comes to your e-commerce site but does not buy anything, for example, then a secondary goal might be to get that visitor to at least subscribe to a newsletter, as this will add a new name to your mailing list.

CRO is the process by which each conversion point is tracked and measured so that it can be improved over time. The conversion point could be the lead magnet, the squeeze page copy, the position of the autoresponder lead capture form (lead form), the design of the page, the thought process of the prospect from the clicking of the ad to the filling of the lead form…basically anything and everything that can be measured about the conversion process.

There are many methods to do CRO, including split testing (A/B testing), multivariate testing, heat maps, focus groups, UI testing, etc.

There are a few points worth remembering about CRO.

* The first step with CRO is that you should gather qualitative and quantitative data before you do any sort of testing. Basically, you do not want to run tests because of what your gut is telling you. You want to base your testing on data, not your gut feeling. Google Analytics will provide you with CRO tools such as Goal Setting, etc.

* The second step is to do A/B tests. When you do A/B testing, you take the original version of your site's squeeze page (known as the control) and then test it against a minor variation (known as the treatment).

 * Do not expect to see increases every single month.

 * You should always optimize for revenue and not optimize for conversions.

 * Drastic changes will always result in drastic results. Once you make a few major changes, you will probably start noticing that things such as button colors will stop having an impact on your conversion rate. Always make small, measurable changes so that they are easier to track.

 * The last lesson is that you need to provide your team with some sort of direction, as they are not miracle workers. Just because you pay them a lot of money to boost your conversions does not mean they will actually be able to do it without any direction from you.

An important point that I wanted to make regarding CRO is that CRO is not a process; it is a mindset — more importantly, it's a *scientific* mindset. You know that CRO is done to improve the profit you make per visitor. So what is it that you are doing to achieve that?

For example, some people add a live chat feature to their websites, but it does not work for everyone. If you decide to put up a live chat feature on your website, your first thought should not be, "Who are the vendors I need to contact? Your first thought should be, "What is the goal/outcome that I hope to achieve by installing a live chat feature on my website?" Your second thought should be, "How can I measure a successful outcome that can be directly attributed to this new feature?" What I am trying to say is don't just implement the latest tactic and think of it as a strategy.

Case Study – Day 13

David starts out Day 13 with another inbox full of emails. He decides to outsource this activity completely by providing his autoresponder login details along with his email account login to his VA, so that he does not need to keep forwarding emails.

When he checks his calendar, he notes that he has five appointments set up for today. Since he would not be able to handle all five appointments, he instructs his VA via email to set up no more than three appointments per day.

After meeting with his three prospects for the day, he receives a call from his PPC consultant mentioning that the weekly budget has been exhausted. David is very disappointed to hear this and asks him why this has happened. The consultant explains that he had set a limit on the expenditure to ensure that David did not go over budget.

David instructs him to pause the AdWords campaign, since he has enough inquiries to handle for now. He also mentions that none of the inquiries on either of the two days have converted to sales. The PPC consultant says that he will look into it.

David calls up his friend Ron, who is also running a Google AdWords campaigns for his own business. Ron advises him to look into all aspects of conversion and not just the lead-to-sale conversion as a metric.

He further explains that there are many different conversions he could look at.
1) Impression-to-Click Ratio (also known as CTR)
2) Click-to-Lead Ratio
3) Lead-to-Appointment Ratio
4) Appointment-to-Sale Ratio

David realizes that there is a lot more to Google AdWords than meets the eye. While the first two items are under the control of his PPC consultant, his VA was in control of the third and he himself was in control of the fourth ratio. However, he was not very happy with the quality of the leads themselves and even though the appointments had been set, the prospects were just looking for free advice and were not looking to sign up with him. In addition to this, his AdWords budget was already exhausted without a single sale for this week.

DAY 14: THE BUYING CYCLE

I mentioned earlier that there is a relationship between content and the sales funnel, and that every single piece of content is an important ingredient of your sales funnel. You need prospects to be attracted to your content in order for your marketing efforts to pay off. (For example, you can attract new visitors via your blog posts and Facebook page.) However, the biggest problem you will face is in knowing how to use your sales funnel in a way that will allow you to beat your competition. In other words, you need to know what type of content to use.

Every single person knows how important content is, and every single person wants his or her content to get all of the attention. People will use catchy headlines with different approaches in order to get their content seen. However, all this really does is create more noise. If you don't take the time to map out your content to the different stages of the buying cycle, you will notice that your content will not deliver the desired result. In other words, it is pointless for your content to have the loudest, weirdest or most creative headline if your content is not actually relevant to the stage of your funnel that your reader is at. As a result, your reader will just skip your content.

There are a hundred different ways you can map out your content to the different stages of the buying cycle. For example, you can use such things as cheat sheets, blog posts, short videos, how-to guides and white papers for the top of your funnel. For the middle of the funnel, you could use longer videos, case studies, e-books, assessments, curated content, webinars, blog posts, or video posts. At the bottom of the funnel, you could use such things as e-zines, case studies, product demos, and in-depth blog posts.

The Consumer Decision Journey

The McKinsey Consulting Group has done extensive research on the sales funnel and customer behavior. They have come out with a report on the "Consumer Decision Journey" based on this research that states that customers now buy using a non-linear approach. What does this mean to you as a marketer? It simply means that you need to map out your content to the various intentions that your potential buyers have.

For example, at the *intent-to-learn* stage, your prospect may not even realize that they have a problem. They are simply at a stage where they want to learn about a new concept that they have heard of. The *intent-to-compare* stage is when your reader knows what their problem is and they start comparing options. Prospects that are at this stage should know what your products offer and how they should use your products.

The *intent-to-order* stage is the stage when your prospects are ready to buy from you and not your competition. They usually know exactly what they are looking for and they usually have their credit cards out, ready to order.

If you learn how to map out your content to readers who have differing intentions, then you will increase your profits.

In order to get started with mapping the buying cycle with the funnel, you need to outline the steps in the process that you require your visitors to take. List every step in the process. After you have compiled the list of actions, evaluate which ones are necessary, which ones can be optimized or combined, and which should be left out entirely.

Case Study – Day 14

David starts out Day 14 by reading the McKinsey report on the "Consumer Decision Journey." He figures that it only takes a click to embark on a journey away from his brand — but on the other hand, it also just takes a single click to come back to his brand. He is worried about not being top-of-mind with his potential customers.

He calls up Ron to discuss it with him. Ron tells him that he simply needs to improve his follow-up and not expect all customers to convert immediately. Ron theorizes that perhaps the initial leads he got were people in the early stages of the buying cycle who were not yet ready to make a payment, since they were evaluating alternatives.

PITSTOP 2

David updates his Success Tracker in Excel with the following details:

Weekly budget, actual: $1200 this week
Leads, actual: 26 leads this week
Appointments, actual: 6 appointments this week
Sales, actual: 0 sales this week

He decides to try his best to catch up with sales, since he does not have any sales yet in the first two weeks.

DAY 15: LEAD SCORING

When you look at your CRM data and your Google AdWords data, you will realize that not all leads are equal. Some are ready to be converted into paying customers, while others aren't ready to buy yet.

It would be a better utilization of your sales resources if you could identify which leads are the hot leads from the many leads that you have generated in other words it's important to determine whether or not a prospect is ready to hear from a sales rep. This can be done via a process called *lead scoring*.

In order to start off with lead scoring, the sales and marketing teams need to work closely together. There are five strategies that should be utilized here:

1. Hold meetings with your sales and marketing teams to determine what characteristics sales-ready leads have. Some of the characteristics that should be taken into consideration here include demographics (i.e., the person's job title, the size of the company, where they're located), what activities they have engaged in while visiting your website, and how you have been able to interact with them. You might even want to select members from both of these teams to

create a new team whose main objective is to continuously be working to better improve such characteristics.

2. The feedback from this meeting needs to be utilized to establish the point value of a sales-ready lead. For example, if the lead were a CEO, then you would assign 10 points to this parameter. If the lead were a COO, then you would assign 5 points to this parameter, and if you cannot determine the designation, then you would assign 1 point to this parameter. Similarly, you need to assign points to all the data collected on your leads.

3. Weighted scores need to be created for different actions. This will require some detective work, as you'll need to review your historical data as well as your existing sales data to see what traits typically help to close a deal. You should also review your marketing automation and website analytics to see what pages were visited, what content was downloaded, and what forms were filled out. In order to become better acclimated with this important marketing information, you may want to establish a spreadsheet that looks at things like email interaction, voluntary requests for information, website visits, information that's been downloaded, and events that have been attended either online or in person.

4. The sales team should take some time to review these proposed scores. Decide which scoring criteria really matter, as some will simply be more important

than others. Once you have determined this, you will be able to set your scoring thresholds. Here, you'll be able to segment leads based upon their scores so that you know who deserves most of your attention. At this stage, you will want to come up with a maximum score of 100 points by assigning the maximum points for the more important data points and prioritizing accordingly. For example, designation of the lead might get a 20% weightage, while the location (within a certain radius) would maybe get a total of 30%, which leaves just 50% to be distributed amongst the other data points.

5. Take some time to test the scoring system against your existing sales pipeline. You'll want to know what the ROI of your lead scoring program is. By tracking and capturing changes, you'll be better equipped to determine your lead-scoring system's true value. Things to look at here include open sales opportunities, any opportunities that have been either unresponsive or unqualified, and leads that are still in the nurturing pipeline. You may need to tweak the percentages here.

You'll never really be done working on your lead-scoring model. Testing and tracking will need to continuously take place in order to identify new ways in which to refine it. Get rid of bad assumptions and remember that as the market is continually evolving, your lead scoring system should also continually be evolving.

Case Study – Day 15

David asks Ron to help him review his website and marketing materials. Ron suggests that David should create more opportunities for the target customer to interact with his brand. As of now there is only one opportunity for each type of customer.

David remembers that his PPC Consultant has asked him to create five more squeeze pages and tells Ron about it. Ron explains that squeeze pages are only one part of the process. While additional squeeze pages would be helpful, they would be better used in conjunction with weighted scores.

He further explains that David might be getting some information from GetResponse regarding his signups. David immediately brightens up and shows Ron the Excel sheet that he has downloaded from GetResponse with his signup data.

Ron shows him that GetResponse is capturing the IP address, postcode, latitude/longitude, city, as well as the campaign name, against each prospect, apart from the name, email address and mobile number that the prospect has entered. He also shows David how he can look up a prospect on Facebook using the mobile number.

David now understands that weighted score simply means assigning some points to each prospect based on the data collected. For example, he can see that there is a prospect from Scotland who has filled out the form, so David assigns him 1 point while assigning 10 points to another prospect who is from Surrey.

They discuss weighted scores in some detail, and also work out a specific number of actions that a typical customer would take before he makes up his mind to do business with David.

DAY 16: AUTORESPONDER

You have already been using your autoresponder for a few days now. Perhaps it is Aweber, GetResponse, or some other similar autoresponder. It is now time to review your autoresponder messages and set up a sequence of pre-written responses. This pre-written sequence is also known as a lead-nurture sequence or a drip-marketing sequence.

A pre-written sequence would follow a delivery schedule similar to the following:

Day 1: First email delivered.
Day 3: Second email delivered.
Day 5: Third email delivered.
Day 8: Fourth email delivered
Immediately after product delivery: Fifth email delivered

Email 1: This will consist of sympathy for their problem and reassurance that you can help.

Email 2: Get "hands-on." Educate them to an understanding of the pain they are feeling; help them to reach the core of the problem at hand.

 # Email 3: Explain that you have an answer for their pain (your product) and proceed to offer it to them.

 # Email 4: Only goes out to people who have not opened Email 3 and asks them if they have seen Email 3.

 # Email 5: A thank-you email for people who take up the offer mentioned in Email 3, outlining the next steps.

As you will note, Email 5 would go out once the prospect purchases the product or signs up for the offer.

Autoresponders are really beneficial because you, as the administrator, sit down one time and do the work that needs to be done. You then set the time sequence you wish to use for delivery, up to a year, and the messages you send through the autoresponder assist you in the marketing and sales aspect.

The purpose of this invaluable tool is to assist you, the company, in building a relationship with those who have subscribed to your list. You do not have to worry about revenue right away; rather, your focus should be that your subscribers read and enjoy the email content you have sent, thus building a solid fan base for your brand.

Autoresponders are used best when they focus on the largest problems subscribers face at that time. Solve one problem with them per message or email. There are various ways to accomplish this:

* You can give PDFs to the subscriber that contains plans and strategies that are easy to implement.

* Take some of your most informative podcasts, articles, and videos and link them to the emails the autoresponder sends for you.

* Sit down and write a quality bio or page of your personal story; this helps subscribers relate to you as a human. Add a photo so they can put a face to your name.

* Offer a page with a common, vexing problem and give the readers a solution to it. This is always a motivator to those familiar with your emails.

* Ask for subscriber support on Facebook, LinkedIn, and Twitter.

How many pre-written emails should you setup in your autoresponder sequence? The answer to this question depends on the following factors:

In a month, how many broadcast messages do you intend to send?
Do you need to bring your market up-to-date?
As far as products you may release in the future, will you rely on them for support?

\# Are you willing to write, and if so, how much?

In general, you should set your autoresponder sequence to last at least 30 days. You will have time to produce quality content, and subscribers will have an opportunity to get to know you during this time. Once this is complete, any subscribers who have signed up for a period of time longer than 30 days should be added to a "broadcast message" list, which I will discuss later.

With all of this made clear, you can then have the choice to create a sequence that consists of a period longer than 30 days. Each message can be written individually and will be sent to each subscriber over the lifetime of the email list you are using. For this very reason, autoresponders are considered invaluable in generating passive income for those who implement them.

Now, keep in mind the importance of sending frequent emails when marketing to new subscribers. You must take care to be certain each email contains content that is of good use to the subscriber. Not only is this valuable to them, but they will come to know the quality of information you send out, and continue to subscribe.

You also may come to realize that different situations call for different frequencies regarding deliveries. Regardless of these differences, always begin with content that has the strongest use and foundation and deliver it within the first two weeks of the subscription. You will slowly begin to deliver the message farther apart, of course, through the passage of time — say, with four- to six-day gaps in between.

Developing & Implementing an Autoresponder Sequence

This is going to be a lot like the planning you would do if you were thinking up the plot of a book. You are going to want to start off asking yourself the theme, or "what is this going to be about?" With that vision, you progress to major scenes or plot lines, chapters and passages, all the way to finally telling a story that fits together fully and completely. It is a step-by-step process that when done correctly will be highly effective and continue to get better responses to your marketing as time passes. Ask yourself, "What do I want my sequence to achieve? What is it I am hoping my subscribers will do as a result of this email? Do I want them to buy? Am I hoping they'll call?"

Now you must do a basic audit of the resources available to you currently. Do you already use resources like infographics, blogs, audio, video, email or other content sources? Implement the resources that will be beneficial to your subscribers. Conduct surveys and case studies that help you to know your subscribers better. Work these things into the email format.

At this point, you should have a fairly impressive

list of topics, as well as many other resources, that can go into your email sequences. You should have abundant resources and boundless ideas for content. On your first sequence, keep it simple: 6-12 emails in the beginning. More can always be added.

Remember:
1) Emails should focus on subscriber goals with the most pressing situation at the time.
2) Add tips and insights into that particular problem. Keep solutions simple at first; you can add more detail as the subscriber foundation strengthens.
3) Balance out the emails you are sending by type or kind. That will ensure a mix of various emails, from those with a sales focus to those of an inspirational nature and more. Just remember, early on, keep them brief.

If you are at this point, I encourage you to sit and plan out your autoresponder sequence.

Case Study – Day 16

David starts out Day 16 by evaluating his current autoresponder sequence. He realizes that he is not really tapping into the pain that the typical landlord is feeling, so he subscribes to the email newsletters of other letting agents so that he can get a better idea of what is out there. He is surprised to see that a few of his competitors have very impressive initial emails that they send out to customers. David gets some better ideas on how to move forward and decides that he needs to sit down and write the autoresponder emails himself.

He dedicates two hours to this activity and is pleased with the results. He creates a total of 20 emails, which he then puts into the autoresponder series.

DAY 17: EMAIL CONTENT

Apart from your autoresponder, you will need to also have a strategy for one-off email messages or for email newsletter messages. There's no right or wrong way to manage a list. All of it simply depends upon your business's long-term goals.

The type of email message you choose to send will depend upon your strategy. Do you want to be aggressive and ask subscribers to spend money? Or do you want to focus on building relationships?

There are only eight types of email tactics. All eight of these tactics serve a different purpose, which you must understand. For instance:

When you're out for the money, focus on a Pure Profit Strategy, using tactics like Agitation, Special Discount, Product Freebie, and Sales emails, whereby you promote products. Make sure to mix them up so that people won't get bored.

When your strategy is to become a Thought Leader/Authority, you'll want to focus on utilizing tactics like Helping Hand, New Content, and Personality emails in order to encourage readers to

consume content and take action.

Hybrid campaigns utilize all of these different types of emails. They usually start with an Authority series before incorporating some Pure Profit strategy emails. Make sure to keep a balance between good content and the occasional promotion.

Let us understand these tactics further.

1) Personality emails provide your subscribers a glimpse into who you are via a short story or anecdote.

2) New Content emails work great when your subscribers are starving for updated information. Herein, you'll want to write 300 words at most and provide links to new content. This works great when you have nothing else to say.

3) Sub-Listing emails are more advanced, as they exist so that you have a way in which to create a more specialized, niche list. They work best whenever you have a second offer that's different from your primary offer. Whenever someone takes action, you can then move them to the other list. Keep these emails around 200 words, simply encouraging readers to take action.

4) Helping Hand emails are where you ask your subscribers to take a specific action. This is a great way to engage your list, since you're asking for input. Herein, you'll need to describe the benefit of the action in 200–300 words.

5) Agitation emails are much more aggressive. Herein, you discuss a problem and its solution. In a future email, you can then solve this problem. Simply write 300–600 words about the problem, then "hint" at a possible solution in the next email.

6) Product Freebie emails expose your readers to new products and encourage them to buy if they like them. Keep these emails short, as you're simply introducing the offer and encouraging them to click a link and check it out.

7) Special Discount emails tie into limited-time offers that expire soon. Hence, it's really a scarcity tactic to help you generate a lot of income by motivating your subscribers to act quickly. As such, they should only be used for time-sensitive offers. They typically follow Agitation messages and serve as a reminder of the deadline. Keep it short and to the point (100–200 words).

8) Sales emails are used in introducing offers and explaining their main benefits. Typically, these are 400 to 800 words long, filled with short, punchy sentences and paragraphs and bullet points.

Case Study – Day 17

David starts working on a calendar for his regular emails so that he can keep his list more engaged with his brand. He decides that he wants to focus on a Thought Leadership strategy for his one-off emails.

The three areas where he wants to establish his thought leadership are Legal Aspects, Passive Income Strategies and Home Improvements. He decides that he really needs to make the time to do this himself. He dedicates three hours to this activity, and at the end he has a total of 26 emails on various topics in these three categories. He also adds some holiday greeting emails to the list, which makes a total of 34 emails in addition to the 20 emails he had written for his autoresponder.

He loads all 34 emails as drafts in the newsletter section of GetResponse.

DAY 18: SEO

Search Engine Optimization (SEO) is a very misunderstood area of digital marketing. Ten years ago, SEO was all about "tricking" search engines to rank your website. But with the advent of Panda, Penguin, and Hummingbird, these tricks no longer work and your site could get penalized by Google; that is, it will no longer rank on Google Search if you or your SEO team use the old bag of tricks.

Most websites will never recover from a Google penalty. Once hit with a Google penalty, you might even need to create a new website!

However, some businesses are still taken in by the tall claims of these tricksters with their "Black-hat SEO" techniques because they claim fast and effective results, like a sprinter. Potential clients should keep their eyes open for those with a "sprinter" mentality. The problem with these sprinters is that sometimes they are able to live up to their claims for the first one or two months before Google shuts them down completely.

The fact is that getting rapid results without a long-term white-hat SEO strategy or a marathon strategy is next to impossible.

The Olympics & SEO: The Parallels

When one is competing in a marathon, one will undergo hours of training, not just to run, but to build up the other parts of the body in preparation for the big race. The training regimen of a sprint runner would probably be as exhaustive; however, a competitive sprint runner would have a very hard time winning a marathon and vice versa. What you produce is what you have been trained, or programmed, to produce. The sprinter has been trained expressly for rapid results; it is that simple.

SEO is a similar type of situation. You have SEO "sprinters." They promise results, fast and easy, and they may even produce them! But their results will have a very short lifespan. The problem is obvious: Now you have been penalized, and it's too late to redeem your website, which means that you have traded short-term success for a long-term failure.

You have to focus on results that are going to be consistent. Consistency is at the very core of SEO success, as it shows dependability and stability, which are the focus here. Long-term planning in regard to SEO, long-term planning as in "marathon" marketing, will not only give you the ability to start the race, but you will be able to carry on consistently through it as well, getting you through right until the end. This type of marketing is what you need for the SEO of your website.

Because of the vast number of competitors in the online field, you should study others whose core business is online; that is, they need their websites for sales of their products or services. Observe their use of SEO and their websites and try to draw comparisons between their strategies and your own. What are the ideas you can borrow from them to improve your own SEO strategy?

When considering SEO, remember this: You want to be around in the long run. Keeping current, planning ahead, frequent reviews and rewrites, and alterations should be completed on an as-needed basis.

How do you identify if your SEO team is using such tactics?

If your SEO team advocates things like keyword stuffing, invisible text, irrelevant keywords, or creating webpages that redirect visitors to another page or using backlinks from link farms, you can be sure that they are using black-hat techniques. If they promise you a specific number of guaranteed links or directory submissions, article spinning and guest posting, or a delivery time for specific results (example: you'll rank #1 within 30 days), you should pay extra attention because it is almost guaranteed that they are using techniques which could get you blacklisted by Google.

If these terms sound too technical or confusing, here are some simple things to beware of…

\# A team that promises you quick results within one to two months

\# Changes to the text of your website to such an extent that the content becomes unreadable or meaningless

\# If you do a web search for your keywords, finding websites with links back to not only your website, but to other websites as well

Case Study – Day 18

David starts out Day 18 by contacting his SEO project manager to discuss the progress up till now. His SEO manager explains that it will take some time to get some traction on Google. In the meantime, some of his keywords have been getting good results, so he suggests that David should focus on those keywords.

David is not very happy with the conversation, so he calls up Ron to discuss the matter. Ron advises him that he should have a long-term view for SEO and that expecting his SEO team to deliver results immediately might get them to cut corners, which would be detrimental to his business. David points out that surely it is good business sense to expect outcomes from an activity that you have invested money in. Ron agrees with him and suggests that David should have a weekly reporting format with his SEO team to ensure that they are working in line with his strategy and that he should set milestones in terms of tasks to be accomplished and not in terms of ranking in the short term.

Ron emails David his weekly SEO tracker so that David can repurpose it for his own business. David is happy to receive it and immediately modifies the tracker and sends it to his SEO project manager with his expectations for the SEO campaign.

DAY 19: FACEBOOK

I assume you already have a Facebook page and that you are interacting with your fans, uploading pictures, and giving information or providing offers. All of this will create loyalty, retention and branding, but very few businesses are utilizing Facebook to its full potential. In other words, they are not using Facebook for the acquisition of new customers.

Facebook's popularity provides business owners with the opportunity to promote their business online with minimal investment. As such, your digital marketing efforts are not fully utilized if you are not using Facebook ads and apps.

With Facebook, a business can create a powerful social network presence simply by promoting themselves and attracting followers. Facebook allows you to create ads that feature your website. Their layout and management tools are similar to Google AdWords.

When you start using this system, you have to remember that it's about the customer and not about you. Therefore, your ad really needs to talk about your customers' needs and not all about your business.

Facebook has a lot of great tools that will help your business grow if used correctly:

1) Storefront Social is an application that turns your Facebook page into an e-commerce site. This means that you can create your own banner and template, as well as other promotional items, then import products from your online store to your Facebook page.

2) Facebook Promotions help you create campaigns for your fans. This is a great way to host contests, offer coupons, and talk about sweepstakes.

3) The Poll app shares your poll on your brand's wall, thus helping you to acquire a wider audience.

4) TabSite allows you to create a welcome page and content, including images, links and more, for your Facebook page.

5) Power Editor is a free yet very powerful and functional advertising tool that allows you to have complete control over the placement, bidding, and targeting of your ads.

6) Custom Audiences is an application that allows you to target customers and email subscribers even if you don't have a Facebook page.

There are also some really neat things that you can do with Facebook ads:

1) Target people who are having a birthday and offer them either a discount or something free

2) Remind your fans about cool events and promotions

3) Introduce yourself to a new company

4) Build new relationships with key people, such as those who have "CEO" or "president" as part of their job titles

5) Get connected with people who work for newspapers, television stations, or major publications

Use sponsored stories

While all of these marketing tools are great, they're meaningless if you don't know how to track your conversions. Here's where you have to monitor whether or not your ads are actually leading to a specific conversation that will end with a sale.

The problem that I have faced with tracking Facebook ads is that I have not been able to use Bitly for tracking the results. But your Google Analytics account in conjunction with a dedicated squeeze page will be helpful to give you that extra layer of performance tracking and also show how you just how much money you should be spending on Facebook ads.

An additional point here with regard to Bitly tracking: You can still use Bitly click-tracking if you are doing regular posts on your fanpage to supplement the data you are getting from Google Analytics, just not for Facebook ads or sponsored stories.

Case Study – Day 19

David starts out Day 19 by signing up for Facebook ads. He is pleased to know that Facebook also has a remarketing option for their ads. He passes the Facebook login details to his PPC consultant and instructs him to use TabSite to set up a welcome page for his Facebook fanpage before he starts the ad campaign on Facebook.

David also decides to set up a poll using the Poll app and the Birthdays feature to engage his Facebook audience and create some goodwill for himself and his brand.

Today is also the day that David makes his first sale through his digital marketing efforts. He is very pleased and books a spa treatment for himself and his wife.

DAY 20: LINKEDIN

With more than 200 million users throughout the world, LinkedIn is quickly expanding and professionals have much to gain by learning how to use it correctly. LinkedIn is most commonly viewed as a medium for B2B, or business-to-business activities, but it can also be useful for B2C, or business-to-consumer interactions as well.

Companies can benefit from LinkedIn in different ways:

Establish strong organizational brands and personal brands.

Create company profiles that boost brand awareness by reflecting the full range of services and products available.

Enhance brand values by growing individual team recommendations and endorsements and by building product and service recommendations.

Embed videos in corporate or personal profiles in order to provide insights into service features, products,

testimonials, case studies and portfolios.

\# Connect with potential clients in a proactive manner who will, with time, develop a better understanding of your reputation and capabilities so that they connect with you when they are ready to make positive purchasing decisions.

\# Routinely post content that is both high in quality and relevant to the targeted market.

\# Utilize the different options in premium membership to contact and message in a targeted fashion according to your business or marketing objectives, whether by searching for and recruiting qualified talent or sales management among other things.

\# Intelligently use analytics data to spot worthwhile opportunities.

LinkedIn provides a lot of valuable company and individual metrics for targeting. If you have not yet gotten a personal profile, establish one and start the process of creating your online reputation.

You will then be able to establish a company profile, which will serve as a mini-website within LinkedIn (which includes careers for job openings, a home page, and product and service pages as well).

Standard Message Template

Check out this template for a standard message that you can use when someone has added you as a contact on LinkedIn.

Dear <prospectname>,

Thank you for connecting with me! I am writing to check if you would be interested in meeting with me to discuss some mutual benefits.

I understand that you are in the <industryname> industry and that you would probably need help with <something that you can help him with personally> or with <something that your company can help him with professionally>

I am <state role within the company> of <name the company>, (a brief explanation of what the company does. Use this space to list the key benefits of doing business with your company. For example, "Our warehouse and distribution services or manufacturing facilities maintain the highest standards, meet stringent global requirements, and have received approval from several regulatory bodies throughout the world.")

<prospectname>, I would also be pleased to connect you with any of my contacts on my LinkedIn network if you think they would be able help you with your business.

Thanks again for connecting with me. I look forward to hearing back from you.

Sincerely,
Your Name
Company Position
Business Name
Email
Website

Case Study – Day 20

David signs up for a LinkedIn premium account so that he can use the InMail feature to contact prospects in his area. He also starts working on his LinkedIn standard message template so that he can have it ready whenever he connects with prospects.

DAY 21: TWITTER

You need to learn how to market on Twitter because it is a place where you can build a large following and you can get your content out there in front of people.

You can also build a good-sized email list using Twitter, and you can do it quickly.

What Can You Promote via Twitter?

There are various things you can promote on Twitter. You can send your followers to a squeeze page, and you can offer to give them something for free there. You can also send them to a blog post, or you can even just send them to an opt-in form where they will sign up in exchange for a free guide or whatever you want to offer.

You can use twitter hashtags to latch on to a current trend related to your business and drive that traffic to your website.

Don't forget to use tracking URLs, since you are

limited to only 140 characters.

Write Engaging Tweets

When you use Twitter, you will want to make sure to write tweets that are designed to get your followers to engage. You want people to retweet your content.

The great thing about having your content retweeted is that the followers who have tweeted your content will engage their users to share your content. This is because their followers will potentially see your content after they have retweeted it.

Helpful Tools

TweetDeck is software that you download to your computer that helps you manage your Twitter account. Another helpful tool is Klout. Klout actually measures your influence on Twitter, as well as on Facebook.

Traffic And Twitter

There are a few ways you can drive traffic with Twitter. For example, if you have published a blog post, then you can send out a tweet directing your followers to follow the link to your blog post.

Google Alerts and Google Trends are also useful to

find trending topics that you can use to generate traffic back to your website via Twitter.

Many successful people on Twitter post their content to Twitter around four times per day. If you think people will get sick and tired of you tweeting your content, then you can just tweet at different times of the day, or simply delete some of your ineffective tweets.

Retweet Content from Popular People

Another thing you should do is follow influential people on Twitter and retweet their posts to your Twitter feed. Sometimes you will have your own content retweeted by them, and this will drive a bunch of traffic to your site.

Setting Up an Account and Building a Following

Set up a Twitter account, which is very easy to do, and then work on building a following. You will want to run special promotions or give people something for free in exchange for them following you on Twitter. You can give away a free guide or some useful information.

You will find that building a Twitter following is quite easy, and it is fun to do. However, more importantly, Twitter marketing works and it works very well.

Case Study – Day 21

David starts out Day 21 by reading an article by Seth Godin about creating tribes. He realizes that for him, the only tribes that matter are people who are interested in the legal aspects of lettings, Passive Income Rental Strategies, and home improvements for landlords. He creates the appropriate hashtags on Twitter and hands off his list of 34 emails to his virtual assistant so that they can be condensed into 140-character tweets.

He is surprised to receive an Excel sheet with his list of tweets in two hours. He has over 120 tweets on the list. He suggests some changes and color-codes the list using the traffic lights system. Red tweets need to be redone according to his inputs, yellow tweets need slight modifications, and green tweets are good to go.

David makes his second sale today and he is ecstatic! He calls up Ron and they head to the pub for a beer.

PITSTOP 3

David updates his Success Tracker in Excel with the following details:

\# **Weekly budget, actual:** $1200 this week
\# **Leads, actual:** 25 leads this week
\# **Appointments, actual:** 15 appointments this week
\# **Sales, actual:** 2 sales this week

He is pleased that he has achieved two sales this week, which has made up for the lack of sales last week. He looks up his traffic data on Google Analytics and notes that he is getting more traffic on Tuesdays and Wednesdays, so he makes a note to discuss that with his PPC consultant.

DAY 22: PINTEREST

It is easy to assume every online business enterprise is successful; however, experienced marketers know that constant marketing campaigns help to brand a business. Here are valuable ways of increasing your search rank using Pinterest.

\# Choose a unique and professional company name
\# Use the same name on all social media sites
\# Include backlinks to your website using pins
\# People who like your Pinterest post will click on the link, and this automatically generates an increase in website traffic
\# Choose an apt and interesting name for your board to entice readers.
\# Think outside of the box and utilize creative marketing techniques that attract readers.

Take a Unique Approach to Marketing

Customers don't take a second glance at dull boards. Pinterest followers enjoy reading informative and interesting content. People join social media sites for their entertainment value. Create lighthearted content that's fun to read to gather a large Pinterest following. Savvy online marketers already know that the site encourages creativity, so work tirelessly to create fascinating boards that are a joy to read. Every online business wants to promote its goods or services, so market your business using fun boards others are able to relate to. Dreary pictures and businesslike text bores readers.

Pins containing a short description are popular. Describing your pins makes them interesting and a short description gives readers an idea of the content. Experienced marketers use inspirational quotes and beautiful images to enhance their pin boards. Adding unique photographs and catchy text helps to brand a business.

Hashtags are Useful Marketing Tools

Hashtags are not just for Twitter. Adding hashtags to the short descriptions makes the boards easier to track. Following these simple tips will help to market your online business efficiently. Every online business owner needs to reach out to a wide audience. Readers who like your boards will click on the hashtag and view your other posts.

Link Pinterest to Other Social Networking Sites

Online marketers should take advantage of every sound marketing opportunity. Link your Pinterest boards to other social media sites to create more interest. The social network sites are buzzing, and linking your boards to other sites increases web traffic and enhances your search rank.

Use Pinterest widgets to market your products. Learn more about the four main Pinterest widget buttons. The widgets offer a simple but effective way of marketing your brand.

The four Pinterest widgets are:
The follow button
The pin it button
The board widget
The profile widget

Pinterest and other social media networking sites are followed by millions. Amateur online marketers should understand they must take advantage of these busy sites to promote their online business. Fail to market your brand effectively, and your online business venture will fail.

Case Study – Day 22

David decides to use a before-after engagement model for Pinterest. He forages his hard drive for photos of ramshackle houses that have been refurbished by his team and remodeled to fetch better rents. He emails these photos to his graphic designer so that she can combine the best images and enhance them and put up some design elements to highlight the Before and After sections.

DAY 23: GOOGLE PLUS

Google owns Google+, which means that Google+ has huge potential to boost one's page rank and visibility. Even though Google has scaled back its commitment to Google+, as of this writing, I have found that there are still some good SEO benefits to be gained by using Google+. Here are some methods that you can use to leverage Google+ better.

The first thing is to open a Google+ account and activate the Google Authorship feature. This feature allows you to link everything you write and publish on the web in places other than Google+ to your Google+ profile.

Once you do this, your image in the Google+ profile will appear alongside every post of yours that is listed in the search engines. This serves to authenticate your content and adds higher credibility to the same.

There are also other ways you can fully exploit the SEO benefits that Google+ offers.

Think strategic networks, not number of circles. This is important since the more circles you add yourself to, the greater the visibility of your content. These circles can be Friends, Family, Influences, B2C, B2B, etc. But in order for this to be effective, you need to ensure that there is a reason behind every circle you create to ensure a better SEO boost via Google+.

Use hashtags. One can never overemphasize the importance of adding relevant hashtags to your Google+ content. Just as in Twitter, using hashtags will make it easier for others to find your content in Google+. Use hashtags with relevant topics so they are easily found, and you've created an outstanding resource that will get you noticed and will increase traffic to your blog.

Link blog posts to Google+. Every time you publish a new blog post, make sure you make a link to it from your Google+ profile. The idea is the same—once you link it to Google+, all the circles members in your profile will get to see the link and this will increase the SEO potential of your page.

The Google+ posts that receive the most comments are resource-type articles with a lot of links. Those covering Google+ how-to information are heavily shared, along with any tutorials. Write a killer post and link back to your own blog for additional resources.

Use the "Ripples" feature. This is a little known feature offered by Google+ that helps you to identify people who have the largest audience in the platform. Once you identify them and add them to your circles, you can then leverage their popularity and spread in the platform to your own advantage.

These are just some of the ways that you can use Google+ to your advantage. As the platform grows and offers new features, it would be beneficial to your business to stay ahead of the curve by adopting those features.

Case Study – Day 23

David makes two sales today out of the three prospects that he meets with. He is very happy that his digital marketing efforts have borne fruit and decides to increase his budget for the next month so that he can do even better.

He starts off his Google+ research by following the big-name thought leaders and influencers in his industry and commenting on their posts. He uses #CircleSharing to find circle-sharing opportunities and adds a Google+ badge to his website.

He highlights the important keyword phrases in his email content with a view toward attracting the right kind of followers. He emails his virtual assistant to repurpose some of his email newsletter content for Google+ and provides his login details to her so that she can do what's needed.

He focuses on creating strategic circles of landlords

who are interested in legal aspects of lettings, Passive Income Rental Strategies, and home improvements.

DAY 24: HOOTSUITE

HootSuite is a tool referred to as a "Social Media Management System" or a "Social Media Management Dashboard." It is definitely an incredible tool that can save you a lot of time. It helps you keep track of and manage your many social network channels and also syndicate your content. You can monitor what people are saying about your brand and respond instantly. You can also connect all your social media channels together, like other Twitter accounts, your Facebook personal profile and Facebook pages, and your LinkedIn profile.

The advantage to HootSuite is you only have to post once and it will get posted on all your channels, which saves you a lot of time. You can set it up to see other things from your Twitter, Google+, and Facebook accounts, such as direct messages, specific lists, and more. HootSuite also works if you have multiple Twitter accounts, which may be a tactic you would want to use if you are targeting several different target audiences on Twitter.

There are a variety of advantages to having all of your social channels in one place on HootSuite. For instance, you can send one message and have it simultaneously broadcast to all of your profiles and pages, or you can have a message go out to only a few select profiles or pages. You can also use it as a scheduler, so that you don't need to be online all the time. You simply write your message in the message field, and then set a day, time, and network or channels where you want to broadcast. You can even upload your content calendar from a spreadsheet to the scheduler.

You can also use your smartphone to manage your HootSuite account and your dashboard from wherever you are, whenever you want to.

Another great feature is "Drafts." Here, you can save the most common messages that you put out as a template. This is useful so that you don't have to type out generic messages time and again.

There is also an interface to embed your Google Analytics code into HootSuite. You simply click on the gear icon to the right, and it opens an "Advanced" settings window. You then choose "Google Analytics" from the "Add custom URL parameters" drop-down.

Each week, HootSuite sends you an email with a PDF attachment of your click summaries. HootSuite gives you graphs showing:
Number of clicks per day
Geographical information on the people clicking through

\# Top referrers
\# Most popular links

Free Vs. Paid

If you are open to using the paid or the pro features of HootSuite, you can delegate responses to different team members. For example, if you receive 10 mentions in one day, you can delegate each one to a different team member. When a team member is logged in, they'll see which tasks have been allocated to them and not make the mistake of responding to a status that has already been replied to.

Another useful tool is HootSuite's messaging feature, which allows team members to send private messages to each other. This is particularly useful for virtual teams.

Case Study – Day 24

David starts out Day 24 by signing up for HootSuite. He hands off his HootSuite login details to his virtual assistant so that she can set up scheduling for the content.

David has also been noticing an alarming trend regarding his old follow-ups; his virtual assistants have not been able to provide him with detailed reports on them. He emails his team so that they can send him the status of the follow-ups.

DAY 25: LEAD QUALIFICATION

Qualification is the most critical and demanding stage of the sales funnel. In the qualification process, you verify that the prospect has a need for your product, that the prospect sees value in your offering, that there is sufficient budget for a deal, that you have access to the decision-maker, and that there is an agreed-upon timeline for the sales process.

A lead can be qualified by using the BANT approach. BANT is an acronym for *budget*, *authority*, *need*, and *timing*. It helps digital marketers decide which leads are likely to convert immediately. If you gather answers to these four questions at the lead stage, prioritize leads and focus on leads that are likely to convert to immediate sales, you have generated some qualified leads.

Basic leads are useful, but qualifying leads saves time and does not demoralize your sales force. A basic lead is likely to contain limited information, such as a name and an email address. This type of sales lead costs much less than a qualified lead. Basic leads have poor conversion rates, whereas qualified leads offer a superior conversion rate. Business owners looking for a good ROI benefit from gaining qualified leads.

Overall, digital marketing leads deliver results if they are serviced at the right time by either a call center or by the salesperson themselves. Sales professionals who favor the BANT approach realize the importance of asking prospective buyers the right questions. Dedicated salespeople are trained to take control of the meeting and put forth targeted questions. Dropping your sales pitch too early may put the customer on the defensive; ask a few probing questions and you remain firmly in the driver's seat.

Studies have shown that people are likely to purchase from someone they feel able to connect with. Those who work to create an honest pitch are likely to succeed. Good salespeople should be able to tap into people's egos, tune into their emotions, and understand their concerns and frustrations. Teach yourself to ask prospective buyers the right questions and they will provide answers. Gain their trust and you increase your sales prospects.

Outbound Call Center Services

The main goal of the outbound call center is to qualify hot leads that will become new customers. At the core of this approach is a detailed, accurate, and updated database. Using data validation tools to remove incorrect entries and correct mistakes is highly advised. A clear and accurate lead database facilitates a higher conversion rate.

Follow-ups

Not all leads will be ready to buy now. One essential part of a good campaign is a specific follow-up plan for leads who express interest in a product or service. Follow-up phone calls need to be friendly and informative, and outsourcing these tasks to a professional call center is often a smart business decision. Experienced call center personnel are well versed at keeping up customer interest and building rapport, which has a positive impact on any company's bottom line.

Effects of a Poorly-Executed Campaign.

Salespeople typically focus on leads that can be closed immediately, which are known as low-hanging fruit. The reason is that going after new leads takes time, and reviving past customer relations can be assigned a lower priority.

However, the task of follow-up is actually easier and less time-consuming than generating new sales leads. This also presents an opportunity to inform about the latest products and services. Failure to follow up can end up costing revenue in the long run. The outbound call center can assist with this process by setting up an effective follow-up sequence until the lead cycle is completed.

Case Study – Day 25

David starts out Day 25 by studying the follow-up reports sent to him by his virtual assistants. He is not happy with the follow-up that is currently happening, or rather *not* happening. He realizes that due to the number of leads that have been coming in, the virtual assistants have not been focusing on the old leads, just the fresh ones.

He decides to look up some websites of professional call centers in the UK and is shocked to see their rates. He wonders if there could be a better and more cost-effective way to follow up with old leads. Instead of using the BANT approach for qualifying his leads, David decides to map his leads by the "six degrees of separation" model instead. He takes a random sample of leads and puts their mobile numbers into Facebook to check if they are in his network. He is pleased to see that 70% of his leads are two degrees away from him.

He decides to split his virtual assistants into three teams. Team 1 will use his Facebook login credentials and research old leads on Facebook and LinkedIn, creating an Excel sheet with their mutual connections mentioned. They will then message the mutual connections from David's Facebook or LinkedIn accounts, asking for a personal introduction to the prospect.

Team 2 would focus on calling the leads provided by Team 1, and Team 3 would be focused on fresh leads. He creates separate daily reports for each team member, so that he can check their progress.

David hopes that this new setup will result in more leads without breaking the bank.

DAY 26: REPORTS

Productivity is measured by the regularity of reports from staff and not by the size of your virtual team. You need to keep your team on track. Keeping them moving in the right direction will greatly benefit your business. However, your monitoring of your team should be kept under control. These benefits won't be accomplished by being a virtual vulture; you'll get them by setting up better systems and control structures.

So instead of breathing down your team's necks, list your recurring tasks and indicate major projects that should be prioritized in a shared calendar, which could be in a project-management system like Basecamp or on an online calendar (*e.g.*, Google Calendar), and then create a reporting process.

Less Work

Usually, when the topic of reporting is brought up, people think they have to do more work. But the truth is an effective reporting can save you from additional work. With effective reporting, you can:

\# Motivate virtual staff to make measurable progress daily

\# Answer questions or bring up problems encountered and
\# Think up new ways to do things better.

A reporting process helps evaluate your team's performance. So at the end of every workday for the first thirty days of a new virtual assistant's employment, have him or her send a report answering the following questions:

\# *What did you accomplish today?* –
This creates a sense of accountability, having to answer this each day.
\# *Is there anything you need help with?* –
This provides a safe forum for your virtual assistant (VA) to ask for help.
\# *Do you have any suggestions or questions?* –
A new VA's suggestions can provide a different perspective and valuable insight on your business.

Paradigm Shift

Most small business owners focus on deficit-based thinking — the gaps and weaknesses, what's wrong, and what's not working. But to see opportunities, a more positive approach must be done: Think in terms of assets, rather than deficits.

Instead of thinking, "That won't work," turn things around and ask, "What could work?" Or if someone did not complete a task, instead of asking, "Why didn't you…?" ask them, "What was in your way?" A different question provides a different perspective.

Every day, there is an opportunity to choose how you perceive a situation, whether big or small. By changing the way you look at things, you can change the way you perceive, filter, and interpret the situation.

A word of caution: Sometimes, it is really easy to just focus on the problems and think about what went wrong rather than looking at what can be learned and gained from a situation. Rather than moan and grumble about how bad the problem is, focus on the solution instead. This changes your own attitude and thinking, and will lead your virtual assistants in the same direction as well.

Other Reports

In addition to reports from your virtual staff, you also have rich reports from Google Analytics, HootSuite, Google Ads, Facebook Ads, and Bitly, to name a few. The trick is to view these reports on a weekly basis with at least one other person and bounce ideas off of each other about what is going well and what needs to improve.

Case Study – Day 26

David starts out Day 26 by evaluating the reports he received from his virtual assistants. He schedules Skype calls with each of them to understand their challenges and makes detailed notes about each interaction.

He decides that he needs to modify each type of report:

For his SEO team, he decides to focus on "proof." In other words, it should be heavy qualitative data mentioning the purpose of the activity, with specific URLs for each linkbuilding activity.

For his telecalling Team 1, he decides to focus on quality of customer profiles and number of profiles built by each team member.

For his telecalling Team 2, he decides to focus on number of calling attempts on the data, quality of call notes, and lead-to-appointment conversion ratios.

For his telecalling Team 3, he also decides to focus on number of attempts made, quality of call notes, and lead-to-appointment conversion ratios.

For his PPC team, he decides to focus on the impression-to-click Ratio, click-to-lead ratio, and percentage of improvement over previous week for lead numbers.

DAY 27: BRAND AND NON-BRAND

There's a great debate over whether or not a company should bid upon their own brand name whenever it comes to PPC marketing. Reasonable arguments can be made both for and against the issue.

Some of the advantages to bidding upon such keywords include:
1) You will have more control over your prospect's journey.
2) It's faster and easier to get updated information out to your client when they come directly to you for information.
3) This traffic isn't easily distracted and is a lot less likely to leave if some part of your website isn't as appealing as they'd hoped it would be.
4) It's less likely that your competition will steal your visitors from you.
5) If you don't bid on branding, your competitors will find it easier to do so, which is obviously something you don't want to let happen.

Your company's brand is defined by a variety of things, including:
1) The people who make up the company
2) Your clients or customers

3) Your company's mission
4) Your company's message

All of this information goes into deciding when your brand should go to market and how. Of course, when it comes to PPC marketing, you want to be as loud as possible because this form of marketing is really effective.

It's important to understand that branded clicks and traffic aren't that expensive in the greater scope of things. Typically, they will only cost you a few cents per click. However, they do lead to a fairly productive conversion production rate.

So, if your competition is bidding on your branding terms, you should be bidding on them, too. Even if your organic listings are doing quite well within the SERPs, you'll want to have your name out there as much as possible. From here on in, your goal should be for your customers to see both your PPC and organic listings in close proximity to one another with a similar message from both.

Regardless of what you do, you shouldn't run tests in regard to the effectiveness of branded PPC traffic and then compare its profitability to that of unpaid-for traffic. It's as if you are comparing apples to oranges, even though the results will always show that it's worthwhile to pay for traffic. Instead, there are some specific metrics that you should be monitoring. For instance, you'll want to take a look at your traffic and if it has decreased in relation to historical data. You'll also want to take a look at your conversions and if organic branded conversions have increased.

It's also important to keep an eye on your competition. If they're actively bidding on your branded terms, then your competition is serving as an active threat to your market share. A lot of people are going to click on competitors' ads, and that's not what you want them to do. You want all of the traffic to come to your site, so you have to determine the best way to get it there.

Case Study – Day 27

David is able to get a sale from all three appointments for the day. He has been observing the trend of his Google AdWords and Facebook ad results, and he notes that the brand-based keywords have been getting a better conversion result in terms of actual sales. He discusses it with Ron, who suggests that perhaps this is because the people looking for his brand name have already decided that they want to buy from him — they have already done their research and they are convinced.

DAY 28: MEASURE

It's important to get a lot of traffic to your website. However, this won't tell you how effectively your website is converting this traffic into paying customers. In order to determine that, you'll need to look at conversion rates.

In order to calculate your conversion rate, simply divide the number of leads by the number of visitors you have. This is what's known as the *visitor-to-lead percentage*. It can be used to determine how many visits you'll need to have in order to reach your goal. If you have a high conversion rate, you'll need fewer visitors. So while it's important to increase traffic to your website, it's even more important to improve upon your conversion rates.

There are a number of factors that can impact your visit-to-lead rate. These include:
1) Your call to action
2) How many landing pages and forms you have out there
3) The quality of your website's content
4) How well your website is designed
5) How good the traffic is that you have coming to your website and where it comes from

You may also want to take a look at what's known as the *lead-to-sale* conversion rate. This is the percentage of leads that become actual customers. It's more difficult to evaluate, since a lot of offline factors also impact it (*e.g.*, your product's quality, your sales team's effectiveness, your business's reputation). Some things that can impact this rate include:

1) Emails
2) Automated workflow
3) Lead scoring
4) CRM Integrations

Conversions play an important role in driving leads and sales. However, they're more effective whenever they're used as part of a strategy instead of a goal in and of themselves. This rate is actually easy to measure if you're using Facebook thanks to their Conversion Measurement tool, which allows you to see exactly which of your Facebook ads result in conversions. All you have to do is put a small bit of code onto your website, and in turn Facebook will show you how your users act once they click on your ad.

Combining conversion measurement with another one of Facebook's tools, which is known as Optimized CPM (OCPM), allows you to get even more targeted with your advertising. Facebook estimates that their tools will help you save approximately 40%.

There are three ways in which these new features

can help you to improve your Facebook ad strategy:

1) You'll be able to track whether someone who seen your ad on their mobile device will later look at it on their desktop computer and vice versa.

2) You'll be able to reduce your cost per conversion by creating more targeted ad campaigns.

3) You'll be able to cut ad spending that isn't providing you with high-value user action.

If you're already highly focused when it comes to Facebook ad targeting, these tools will help you create even better campaigns. Their calls to action and URLs will lead your customers to take action as you stand by to track the results.

Case Study – Day 28

David starts out Day 28 by studying the Google conversion codes and Facebook OCPM. He decides to focus his efforts on the visit-to-lead ratio, starting by reviewing the call-to-action buttons and the landing pages. He also decides that he needs to add another freelancer to his team who can focus on editing and proofreading the content.

Reviewing all the traffic sources from his Bitly stats, David notes that most of his traffic is coming in from his social media activities.

PITSTOP 4

David updates his Success Tracker in Excel with the following details:

Weekly budget, actual: $1200 this week
Leads, actual: 25 leads this week
Appointments, actual: 15 appointments this week
Sales, actual: 5 sales this week

He is pleased that he has achieved 5 sales this week and a total of 76 leads have been generated this month from his digital marketing efforts. He decides to look into his Bitly account to check for trends in his traffic sources. He follows the following steps.

1) He logs into his Bitly.com account.
2) He finds the first link that shows clicks and clicks on the View Stats for that link.
3) He notices that he gets more clicks on Tuesdays and Wednesdays.
4) He also makes a note of when his links were shared and looks for patterns within the Geographic Distribution of Clicks.
5) He repeats this statistics check with each of his

Bitly links.

After some time checking out these stats, he starts to get a little tired, but then he reminds himself that he is just looking for patterns and does not need to set up an action item for each one. From what he has seen so far, it is obvious that his marketing methods are working, so he is pleased with that.

DAY 29: CUSTOMER BEHAVIOR

It is a fact that marketing tactics boost conversions. There is a whole industry based on studying customer behavior to come up with insights that can help understand the buying cycle.

What is meant by "the buying cycle?" This is the process customers use before making a final purchase.

The Five Stages of the Customer Buying Cycle

Customer Awareness: Prospective customers identify a need and realize that your business can fulfill their need.
Consideration: The customer weighs the options by checking similar items offered on other websites.
Intent and Preference: Customer behavior indicates they use both logic and emotion before making a purchase.
Purchase: The customer orders goods from your e-commerce site.
Repurchase: Contented purchasers utilize logical and emotional processes that lead to repurchase.

To understand the Customer Buying Cycle better, marketers should study search trends. Here are a few examples of current customer search trends:

Flat screen TV – Customers who are considering purchasing a flat screen television carry out a generic search. The nature of the query itself shows us that the prospect is not yet ready to buy.

Compare flat screen TVs – Prospective buyers try to compare alternatives. The nature of the query shows us that even though they seem to have a genuine requirement, they have not yet made up their mind.

Sony 42 inch LCD – The customer is stating a preference and is ready to buy, but perhaps has not yet decided who he should buy from.

Online business owners should focus on building a dependable customer pipeline. Since all prospects are at different stages of the buying cycle, you should not treat everyone as if they were ready to buy. Therefore, follow-up becomes crucial.

The majority of customers locate e-commerce websites via search engine marketing. Pay-per-click (PPC) and search engine optimization are valuable online marketing strategies. In addition to this, the content on your website should be geared towards selling your products or services.

Recent customer behavior studies show that buyers look for coupons and discounts. These offers can be created through a pre-sales email or a PPC advertisement. Customers like to deal with friendly and trusted sellers, therefore you should keep contact with valued customers via social media sites, personal outreach, and scheduled emails.

Here are some more tactics that can work for you:

\# Provide spec sheets that inform customers about your brand
\# Use customer testimonials to your advantage
\# Add exciting content that encourages shoppers to buy
\# Offer a limited-time discount
\# Send monthly newsletters that entice them to repurchase
\# Use the right traffic sources to make content available

Business owners and marketers who research their market, draw up unique marketing plans, and implement the five stage customer buying cycle stay ahead of the game. Marketers who fail to consider customer behavior tend to fall at the first hurdle.

Case Study – Day 29

David starts out Day 29 by studying the Google Analytics account to check how many of his customers are coming in from mobile devices. He is pleasantly surprised to find that 40% of customers are visiting his website from mobile devices and tablets. He realizes that his landing pages are not optimized for mobile devices, and that could perhaps result in some loss of revenue.

He also decides to pause some Google AdWords campaigns that have not resulted in a good visit-to-lead ratio.

DAY 30: THE REVIEW

Once you have an established business that's running well, you need to review your plans and start making new ones. Here you'll want to determine how you can make the most out of the market position that you've been able to establish. You'll also want to decide upon some new goals for your business. This is simply a part of revisiting and updating your business plan.

It's important to put some effort into long-term, strategic planning. This is especially true if you're unsure about:

1) How your business is performing
2) If you're getting the most out of your business
3) If you're making the most of the opportunities that are presenting themselves to you
4) Whether or not your business plan is outdated
5) Why your business is moving in a different direction than you had anticipated
6) Why the business is unresponsive to the market's demands

A marketing review is also useful whenever you're

establishing the direction for your company. This is because it will provide you with answers to:

1) What direction should the business be heading in?
2) What markets should I be competing in?
3) What resources are necessary for successfully competing within these markets?
4) What facilities are necessary for successfully competing within these markets?
5) What type of business environment are we competing in?
6) What's changed since I started my business?
7) What external factors are affecting my business's ability to compete?
8) How's my business's success being measured?

You may need some help from senior staff in your business to answer these questions. They will be able to help you assess your core activities to see how effectively you're meeting your customers' needs. You should also consider which products and services are succeeding, as well as why the others aren't performing as planned. The answers to these questions form the basis upon which your business's improved performance and profitability rests.

Some other things that you should take a look at include:

1) Your business's location
2) The facilities that your business is operating out

of
3) How you're handling information technology
4) The people that you have in place and what their skills are
5) Your financial position

While all of things mentioned above are important when you're reviewing your business plan, the way in which you conduct the review is equally important. There are a variety of useful business-analysis models available for you to choose from.

1) The SWOT analysis is by far the most popular. It takes a look at your business' strengths, weaknesses, opportunities, and threats.

2) The STEEPLE analysis helps you understand the various external influences upon your business, whether they be social, technological, economical, environmental, political, legal, or ethical.

3) Scenario planning helps take a look at the future of the business.

4) Critical success factor analysis is used to identify the areas in which a business needs to succeed in order to be able to achieve its objectives.

5) The Five Forces looks at five factors that influence the development of markets and businesses.

Case Study – Day 30

David calls up Ron to ask if they could meet up for a cup of coffee. David wants to get Ron's inputs on his marketing campaigns and what he could do going forward.

He shows Ron the report formats that he has come up with to track the effectiveness of his team. Ron suggests that he will probably require another salesperson, since the number of appointments has gone up. Ron suggests a commission-only sales person.

Also, David asks Ron if the business model needs to be changed. Ron suggests that perhaps David is thinking too small. David agrees and says that he has been wondering about that, too. Now that he is established as a thought leader on lettings in the Surrey area, nothing should prevent him from being established as a thought leader throughout the UK, but that would probably mean changing the business model itself.

Ron suggests that perhaps that would not be required at all. All he would need to do would be to look at this as a different business, altogether separate from PI Rentals. David likes the idea and asks Ron if he would like to be a partner in his new venture. Ron is pleased, but says that he would need at least a week to think about it.

The two friends sip their coffee and recount how hectic the last 30 days have been. David is thrilled with the new direction and the new ideas that they have discussed. He can hardly wait for next week, when they plan to meet again.

SECTION 3

YOU'VE FINISHED THE BOOK. NOW WHAT?

Digital marketing doesn't have to be a difficult process, but I would not claim that it is super-easy. The good news is that you can do it if you work toward it on a daily basis. It all comes down to dedicating yourself to the process.

In this book, you've learned several new ways to generate new leads for your business. So it's time to take action!

Start out small. Use the techniques given to outsource if required — the idea is not to try to do it all by yourself.

Don't be afraid of making mistakes. Just be sure that you learn from each experience and use this information to move forward.

If you want to make big changes in your marketing, you're going to need help. No need to worry. You won't have to do it alone, even if you don't have the budget for a team. I have created a website, http://www.authorandfriend.com/brief/, where you'll get exclusive access to additional content, helpful checklists and templates on each of the sections we have covered, and more!

The important thing to remember is that you can learn anything. Whenever you get stuck with a specific topic, simply do a search on Google or YouTube. Both websites have a wealth of information that can help you overcome any obstacle.

Now, it's up to you!

Don't just close this book. Immediately apply what you've just learned. To help you further, I have listed the resources you will need along the way in the next section.

I wish you success and all the best.

LIST OF RESOURCES

http://bit.ly/1qKCLK6 - GetResponse - 30 day Trial Available
Autoresponder Software

http://bit.ly/1viZZqC - SEO Link Monster
SEO Link Building System

http://bit.ly/1o06Rok - Mailchimp
Email Newsletter Software

http://bit.ly/RK3lmR - Aweber Autoresponder
Autoresponder Software

https://bitly.com/ Bitly
URL tracking system and measurement tool

http://bit.ly/1jTAOpW Keyword Spy Software
Spy on your competitors – competitive keyword software for SEO

COMMUNICATION TOOLS REQUIRED FOR A VIRTUAL TEAM

http://bit.ly/1mHWEx7 Dropbox
For sharing files with your virtual team

http://bit.ly/1jVQhWx Basecamp
For managing multiple projects

http://bit.ly/1n6HOmJ Nimble
Free CRM system for up to 3000 contacts

http://bit.ly/1gDuP9i Elance
Job-posting marketplace for freelancing virtual assistants

http://bit.ly/1ke6hmr Freelancer.com
Large job-posting marketplace with many international freelancers

http://bit.ly/1vnrgIg Odesk
Job-posting marketplace for freelancing virtual assistants

LIST OF FREELANCERS (TEAM MEMBERS REQUIRED)

Analytics Manager/Excel Expert
Telecallers/Appointment setters
Content Writer
Graphic Designer
Webmaster
Video Editing specialist
PPC Consultant
SEO Consultant

You can also categorize in the following manner

- # Technical
- # Analytical
- # Creative
- # Content
- # Auditors
- # Product Creators

MORE KINDLE BOOKS BY ROMUALD ANDRADE

Please click the link below to check out my other books

http://www.amazon.com/Romuald-Andrade/e/B00J272LEU/

Printed in Great Britain
by Amazon